THE MISSION OF SAINT MUNGO

THE MISSION OF SAINT MUNGO

John Glass

ATHENA PRESS
LONDON

THE MISSION OF SAINT MUNGO
Copyright © John Glass 2007

All Rights Reserved

No part of this book may be reproduced in any form
by photocopying or by any electronic or mechanical means,
including information storage or retrieval systems,
without permission in writing from both the copyright
owner and the publisher of this book.

ISBN 10-digit: 1 84401 822 9
ISBN 13-digit: 978 1 84401 822 2

First Published 2007 by
ATHENA PRESS
Queen's House, 2 Holly Road
Twickenham TW1 4EG
United Kingdom

Printed for Athena Press

I dedicate this book to the memory of the Rev. Fr James Wallace, 1933–2005, without whose encouragement I may not have completed this book.

SAINT KENTIGERN MUNGO

*Saint Mungo,
first bishop of Glasgow and Scotland,
patron saint of Glasgow and Alloa.*

Introduction

The following story of Saint Mungo, which I have put down to paper, has been inspired in part by I G Capaldi, SJ's *Tales of Kentigern*, which he, in turn, had adapted from a book written some 800 years ago by a Cistercian monk called Jocelyn of Furness. In these pages I have tried to paint a more human face for our patron saint in my own words.

History, legend and folklore – that's the life of Saint Mungo, or, as he is also known, Kentigern. There is little record of Mungo until around the year 1174, when Jocelyn of Furness Abbey put pen to paper and wrote a book in Latin called *Vita Kentigerni*. This book was translated into English; from then on, most stories of Saint Mungo have come about as a direct result of this one book. It is not known who was first to translate this book into written English, but Capaldi's book is one of the last to have tried to make sense of the Latin book.

Jocelyn is possibly the one nearest to the truth about Saint Mungo since he is nearest in time. I was once told that folklore and legends are 50 per cent truth and 50 per cent fiction. With that in mind, we can still be fairly certain that he was born near Culross around the year 518 and left on a mission to Glasgow after his consecration at the age of twenty-five years old. His life thereafter was filled with his devotion to the Lord and his moral excellence in the evangelising and the conversion of the pagan tribes. His death, at the age of eighty-five, was on 13 January 603. His festival is still kept throughout Scotland on this date.

My own quest was to find the link which binds Saint Mungo with Alloa, where a church, the history of which goes back to around the tenth century, has been dedicated to him. It is with no apology from me that I have taken poetic licence with the following stories about Saint Mungo, although I have tried to stay true as much as possible to what has been written before about our venerated saint. I have tried to use local knowledge and facts that were not available to

Jocelyn in his day. I have also tried to fill in the missing part of Saint Mungo's life between leaving Culross and his meeting with an old man called Fergus at Carnock, who was later known as Saint Fergus. There is a reference (on p.44 in W Stephen's *A History of the Scottish Church*) as to how Saint Mungo crossed the River Forth – Stephens writes, 'Kentigern travels westward by the shores of the Friesian Sea, believed to be the Forth, and here he is stopped by the River Mallena.' He goes on to say: 'The Mallena changed its channel and flowed back into the River Ledone.'

In the *Vita Kentigerni* Jocelyn states that Saint Mungo parted the water where the Mallena meets the Ledone; these two words have been translated as the Rivers Forth and Teith. In Latin, these words actually mean 'flood' and 'ebb tide', and could relate to the tide of the Forth any place from the Inche island at Alloa and on down the Forth to Limekillins in Fife. Fishermen of old in these parts have always known about a tide that they called the Leaky. A ballad called 'The Leaky' was published some 300 years ago based on the folklore about our saint and his altercation with the Forth. This ballad can be read in a book written by John Crawford called *The Memorials of Alloa*, which can be found in the Alloa Library. Folklore has attributed this phenomenon to a miracle performed by Saint Mungo when he crossed over the River Forth. It is also local knowledge that the River Forth near Alloa has a ford at low tide, and the Roman Army had an outpost on Mars Hill (possibly named after the Roman god of war). These findings have led me to believe that Saint Mungo may well have crossed over the River Forth at Alloa. If he did then the local people of that time may have witnessed this great miracle, hence the dedication of this land to our venerated saint.

In researching Saint Mungo's life and the history of that time, along with a study of the geology of the land and the rivers, I have been taken to places in history that have stimulated me to carry the story of his life further: his trials in the Strathclyde area; his travels and his setting up of monasteries in Cumbria; the legends of his being confessor and confidante to leaders of that time; meetings with Saint David, the King of Wales and King Arthur of the Round Table, Saint Columba and other legendary people who drift in and out of our patron saint's life.

Economically, places where Saint Mungo established or stayed for a time, or, more importantly, performed a miracle all in time became the most important towns of their areas: places like Culross, Alloa, Glasgow, Carlisle and Llanelwy (modern name, Saint Asaph) in Wales and many others. Is it coincidence that a number of these places have suffered a downturn in their fortune? Maybe not. Maybe it is because we have all forgotten what our patron saint left for us in his teachings.

I hope my journey of discovering Saint Mungo will also be your own journey and lead you to a better understanding of this great saint whose name, Kentigern, means 'head priest': head above all others.

Acknowledgements

Thank you to Dunfermline Carnegie Library, for all the assistance they afforded me.
Alloa Library, for their assistance and advice.
National Map Library of Scotland.

Contents

Summi Pontifces	13
The Saint who was called Mungo	15
The Legend of Saint Thenew	23
The Miracle of the Little Robin	24
The Hazel Catkin Holy Flames	28
The Growing Years of Mungo	35
The Monastery Cook	44
The Journey begins	49
Mungo's Journey with Saint Fergus	63
Dear Green Place, Glashgu	68
The Glashgu Mission	75
Mungo faces his Foe	83
Conquering of Doubts	90
Mungo's Mission South	95
Meeting Saint David (Dewi)	101
Mungo's Prodigy, Asaph	108
The Battle of Ardderyd	115
The Journey Home	121
The Ring of Truth	129
The Meeting of Saints	136
The Final Journey	142
Select Bibliography	149

Scotland in the sixth century

Summi Pontifces

Popes on the Seat of Peter during the life of Saint Mungo

514–523 Saint Hormisda
523–526 Saint Ioannes I
526–530 Saint Felix IV
530–532 Donifacius II
533–535 Ioannes II
535–536 Saint Agapitus
536–537 Saint Silverius
537–555 Saint Vigilius
556–561 Saint Pelagius I
561–574 Saint Ioannes III
574–579 Saint Benedictus I
579–590 Saint Pelagius II
590–604 Saint Gregorius I (Gregory)

The Saint who was called Mungo

Saint Mungo. That is a name we have all heard, but I wonder how many of us really know who Saint Mungo was. Most scribes will tell us Saint Mungo was born around the year AD 518, near Culross in Fife. He 'is believed to have been born' the illegitimate son of a princess of the Angle race, whose name was either Thenew or Thaneit. She was the daughter of King Lothus, who was ruler of the kingdom of Lothian.

To try to understand the man who became a saint, we have to go back to a time before he was born. The Scotland we know today was a very different place long, long ago. Around about the year AD 220, the great Roman legions withdrew south – from the protection of the Antonine Wall, which stretched all the way from Boness on the River Forth westwards to old Kilpatrick on the River Clyde – back behind Hadrian's Wall. This left a vacuum of power in the region, and over the next 270 years a struggle for supremacy took place; small tribes were conquered and land confiscated, until fewer, but larger, kingdoms were left. Around this time the Pict tribes controlled the land to the north of the two great rivers Forth and Clyde; the land to the east and south-east was under the control of the Angles. Along the Clyde valley the Briton tribes remained the dominant force. To the south-west of the Cambrian kingdom the marauding armies of the Gaels caused havoc by pillage and plunder. During this period, most of the different tribes were pagan, except for a small scattering of Christians. The Druids had looked after their superstitions and religious well-being for aeons.

With the coming of Christianity, some of the tribes embraced a loose kind of Christian faith, but only the Britons, the tribes that controlled most of the area either side of the River Clyde in the Strathclyde region, had embraced a deeper Christian faith. It is thought that the Britons may have been allies of the Roman legions and had embraced the Christian faith from them. They may have also fought alongside their Roman conquerors. When

Christianity started to spread, it may have been felt that it was better to integrate the new beliefs into Druidic culture, rather than completely try to change things overnight. This meant that their new Christian faith had to be continually evangelised. The Pict tribes, though, wanted to hang on to their old ways. They were more stubborn and had not embraced the faith; their rule of law was the survival of the fittest where brutal pagan leaders of the races were always spoiling for a fight. Life and death struggles in the pagan-controlled areas were pretty much the order of the day, and powerful pagan chiefs gradually came to control larger areas. Scotland's map was beginning to settle.

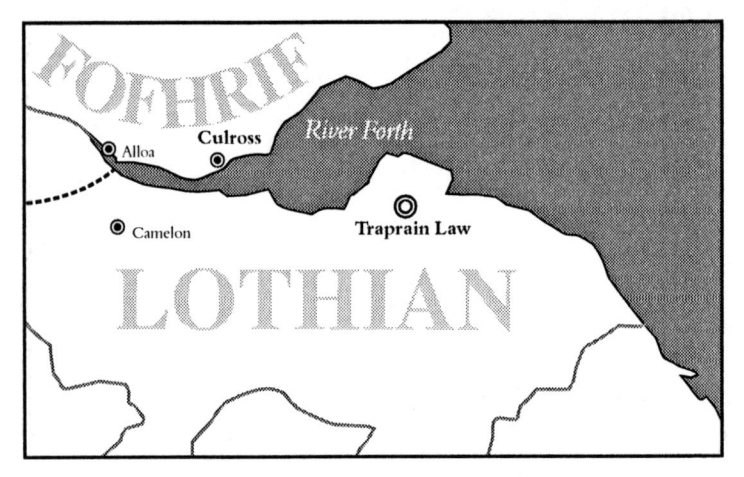

The kingdom of King Lothus

To start our journey, we have to go back in time, to around the year AD 517, to a land south of the great River Forth. This land was named Lothian after its leader, who, history tells us, was a brutal, barbaric man by the name of Lothus, king of the Angles. His fortress was on a hill in the East Lothian called Traprain Law (markings of his fort can still be seen there to this day). His kingdom stretched from the River Forth, all the way down the east of Scotland into the very heart of Yorkshire.

In those days there was a continual struggle for power and, in order to maintain control of such a vast kingdom, King Lothus was forever away repelling raiders of other tribes, fighting battles to maintain the power over his domain, and expanding his kingdom into new territory. It was during one of these campaigns that our story begins.

Traprain Law, the fortress of King Lothus

Before King Lothus left to resolve a matter in another part of his kingdom, he ordered his squires and young warrior princes to guard and protect his wives and daughters. Legend has it that at this time a young, innocent girl, Princess Thenew, daughter of Lothus, refused to marry the suitor of the King's choosing. Angry at her refusal, this same suitor abducted her and, held against her will, she was degraded and abused, her innocence damaged. She was later returned to her family. So the legend goes.

Or it may have been that the girl's infatuation with one of the young princes, who had been entrusted to guard the King's closest family, led to something more. It would have been the perfect opportunity for this young prince, while his master was away, to take advantage of her innocence. In either case, according to legend, the outcome of this was that she was raped and found to be with child. Because she was so young and very innocent, it is thought some of the household may have helped to keep her secret for a while from the King's men.

King Lothus was a strict man. The penalty for disobeying him was death; even his own nearest family was not exempt from his wrath. He returned some months later, after a long campaign. By this time, rumours abounded and the princess could not hide any longer the fact that she was with child. It was not long before the King found out, and Princess Thenew was summoned to appear before him. When the King saw for himself that the rumour was true, he was consumed by anger at the thought that one of his own daughters would disobey him or allow this to happen – even though she was the innocent in the wrongdoing. King Lothus's arrogance would not let him listen to her plea for mercy.

To show his subjects that his will was law, he sentenced her to be cast off the nearby cliffs on the south side of Traprain Law Hill. His executioners escorted her to the top of the hill and carried out his command, but when they went to verify the outcome, to their amazement, rather than being dead, she was alive! She had hardly a scratch on her, and her unborn baby was miraculously unscathed.

One of the executioners ran back to inform the king, perhaps thinking, as she had survived the fall, that her father would forgive her. To the executioners her survival only reinforced their doubts of her guilt. But their words were to no avail. To the King, the thought of her survival only increased his anger. More determined than ever to impose his will over his subjects, he told the executioners that she was to be thrown into a small coracle boat and cast to the mercy of the River Forth.

By the time they reached the river it was nearly night-time and a cold wind was blowing from the east. The guards looked out over the choppy, dark water and felt glad that it wasn't their

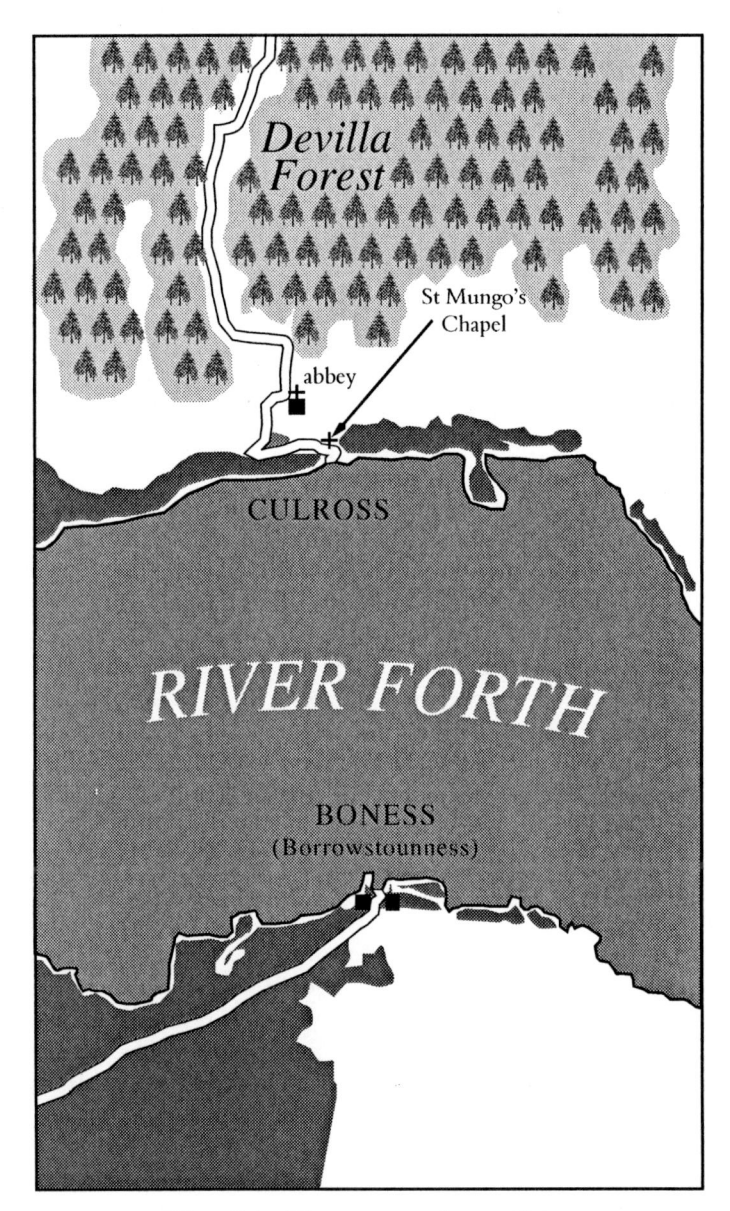

Where Saint Thenew came ashore at Culross

destiny to be cast adrift that night. This time, the executioners carried out their orders in fear. Even though they may have sympathised with the young girl, the penalty that would be imposed on them was far too great to disobey their lord Lothus.

Princess Thenew, who was still with child, was dragged to her fate. They threw her into the small coracle, unceremoniously cast it adrift and left her to her fate, the elements and the fast-flowing tides of the River Forth. As it happened, a guiding hand from above was with her; the tide was flowing inland. Even so, it was a rough crossing. She lay on the floor of the little boat, crying and suffering pain from the first attempt to execute her. She must have missed the comfort of her home, her mother and her friends, worried about her unborn child, and wondered why: why should this be happening to her? For someone so young, it must have been a terrifying ordeal.

The little boat drifted onwards, inland. With the wind and the tide tossing and turning the coracle this way and that way, all she could do was hang on for dear life. Eventually, after what seemed hours, it was driven nearer to the shoreline. At the sight of the river's edge, she relaxed, thinking that her ordeal was nearly over. As fate had it, she was to be disappointed, for on reaching the riverside the oracle crashed on to the rocky shore, spilling her into the water. Struggling against the waves, she managed to pull herself up on to dry land. Cold and wet, she lay there, exhausted. After a while she crawled into a sheltered spot and rested. How long she lay there is conjecture, but during this time, all alone, she gave birth to a baby boy.

At this very same moment, as folklore has it, not too far away in an abbey near Culross a monk by the name of Servanus (Saint Serf) had a premonition that something wonderful had happened. He called all the friars to prayer and told then of his dream that something wonderful was about to enter into their lives. Some time later, some local fishermen returning from a fishing expedition stumbled upon Princess Thenew and her baby. As she was so very weak, they fashioned a stretcher and carried both mother and child the few miles to the abbey. On arrival at the gates, one of the fishermen ran into the abbey and told Servanus about how they had found this young girl with a child.

Before the fisherman had finished telling him of their find, Servanus knew right away that this was what he had dreamed about. He ran out and embraced both mother and child, and, overjoyed, he told her, 'You and your child are both safe now, as it was God's hand that had guided you to me.' Servanus took mother and child into the abbey. The first thoughts of Servanus were for the souls of both mother and child, so he arranged a baptismal service to baptise them into the Christian faith. Calling together the friars, they held a service, singing psalms and praise, thanking the Lord for the safe recovery of this young mother and child. Her ordeal over, Thenew settled in the monastery under the protection of the pious Servanus, where she watched her son grow in the light of the Lord.

It would seem even at birth Saint Mungo was blessed from above, considering he survived the hands of a cruel king, the treacherous waters of the River Forth, a lonely birth in the wild, and, after all that, was delivered into the safe hands of a saintly monk. This pious monk, from that day on till Mungo gained manhood, would be his mentor and help shape the man who one day would become Saint Mungo.

It is believed that it was Servanus who gave Saint Mungo his name. Two names are attributed to Saint Mungo: he is known locally as Mungo and as Kentigern in other parts; but both these names have been attributed to him as his baptismal name. The translation of these two names, though, leads me to believe that when he was baptised he was christened Mungo, which in the local dialect means 'dear one'. The other name, Kentigern, which means 'head priest', may have been given to him much later, after he had established his own order of monks while in Wales. The meaning of these two names has many interpretations. The language of this area of Scotland at that time is not fully known. It is thought that the people of the areas close to the borders spoke a mixture of Celtic languages. As with today, local accents and dialects were thrown in. It is possible Saint Serf may have named his protégé 'Mochohe', (Mungo) which Jocelyn translates into Latin, *'care mi'*, or 'dear one'. For me, this is the name I think suits him best at his baptism: Mungo, 'dear one'.

Statue of Saint Thenew, mother of Saint Mungo. This Victorian statue is now owned by Saint Thenog's Primary School, Garthamlock.

The Legend of Saint Thenew

According to the liturgical references available, Saint Thenew died in Glasgow and her bones were venerated there. One of the burgh gates or ports, situated beside Saint Thenew's chapel on the west of the town, was known as Saint Thenew's gate. There are different pronunciations of the name Thenew, including Thenog, Tannog, Tennoch, Thaneit and Enoch. Her name survives in the place name of Saint Enoch Square. Saint Thenew's day was celebrated on 18 July in the Scottish calendars.

The Miracle of the Little Robin

About Saint Mungo's infancy we can only speculate, but we can be sure that there would have been no safer place to be raised than in the sanctuary of the abbey. Life there would have been very austere for the little infant Mungo, but folklore has it that from a very early age Mungo was taken under the wing of the pious Servanus. So it was that Mungo had a father figure to look up to. Servanus may have taken the infant Mungo into the abbey gardens he loved so much; like a father he would have taught and allowed Mungo to see the real beauty of the nature all around. He would have started telling his young protégé, as soon as he was able to learn, all about the teachings of Jesus. Folklore has it that Servanus looked on Mungo as the very special son he would have liked as his own. Either way, there was a close bond between them which grew stronger with time.

As Mungo grew older it was time for him to join in with the other boys, most of whom were sons of local chieftains in the service of the Lord. They came into the abbey from the surrounding area to be educated and to learn all about the word of Jesus.

Mungo was a very conscientious and willing learner, even at this early age, and this was a cause of some discontent among some of the older boys. Some of the boys were there because of a calling from God, others because they would be fed, but some were there because their parents forced them. Servanus, who adored young Mungo as a son, when giving praise for his ability to grasp the lessons, may unwittingly have been the reason some of the boys were jealous. This jealousy festered until they started to tease and pick on Mungo, who was much younger than they were. He was a very forgiving boy, though, and would often say prayers asking forgiveness for the malice of the boys. It was a cruel prank by some of these boys that led to the first miracle attributed to Saint Mungo.

It all began one day when Servanus was praying. While out walking round the abbey gardens, he befriended a little robin. This little robin would fly around his head and land on his shoulder, and Servanus spent many precious moments when in its company, taking great joy in feeding the little bird out of his hand. Each day thereafter, when Servanus was in the garden, the little robin would come to him. One day, Servanus had finished teaching for the day, and he praised young Mungo for his attentiveness. This did not go down too well with some of the boys and, as a result, they planned to blacken Mungo's good name in Servanus' eyes.

Before Servanus retired into the garden, some boys sneaked in before him, planning to hide the little robin and blame young Mungo. The bird flew down to them, since it was quite tame, and one of the boys caught it in his hand. The boys began to argue about who should hide the robin. They pulled and pushed each other, but suddenly they stopped. The little robin was dead. The robin's head had been torn from its little body.

The prank had gone very wrong. To cover their deed they hid

the body of the robin behind some bushes. When Servanus walked into the garden, the boys, fearing a reprisal for their dastardly deed, and feeling guilty, all shouted as one, 'Mungo killed the little robin!' Servanus was dismayed at the thought of losing his little friend, even more so that it could have been his beloved Mungo who might have carried out this deed. But deep in his heart he could not believe Mungo was guilty.

While the boys crowded around about Servanus, intent on blaming Mungo to save their own skins, they didn't notice Mungo quietly walk over to the dead robin. He picked it up, impressed upon it the sign of the cross, clasped his hands around it, and breathed on the little robin. Then, raising his pure hands in prayer to the Lord, he said, 'Oh Lord Jesus Christ in whose hands is the breath of all Your creatures, rational and irrational, give back to this little bird the breath of life, that Your blessed name be glorified for ever.'

The Lord Jesus Christ, looking upon and favouring Mungo, performed a miracle, and immediately the little bird was restored to life. Just then, Servanus approached. Mungo opened his hand and, lo and behold, the little robin stood up, and flew straight towards Servanus. Servanus was overjoyed that his little friend was alive. The little robin flew round his head, landed on his hand, took some seed, and then flew away. With his own eyes Servanus had seen what his prodigy had done, and the holy man's heart exalted the Lord with praises that the child could have been so blessed by the Lord, for only the Lord alone could have, through this child, worked this marvellous miracle. By this remarkable sign the Lord signified to all that Mungo was one of his chosen own and that the Lord would be watching over him from this day on.

Most of the boys believed what they saw: others would not believe their own eyes and said it was not the same bird, but only a trick. Some, it seems, could not overcome their jealousy, and just gathered more resentment towards Mungo. The next day, when Servanus was in the garden, as every day before, the little robin came to him. Realising some of the boys still resented Mungo and were still not convinced it was his same little robin, Servanus called them over, and, gently pulling back the feathers from around its neck, let them see the mark on its neck where the head had been joined to the body. At this, most then knew it was indeed the same little robin and that Mungo was a very special person in the eyes of God. Some, though, still resisted the truth and swore to get even. They had tried to blacken Mungo's name and had failed. Mungo sensed this and, taking pity, he prayed for them. It was his way was to forgive rather than accuse.

Miracles, it would seem, come in all sizes. Even the smallest ones, when they happen – even to ourselves, when we see them with our own eyes – are sometimes hard to believe: a tree bursting into life in the springtime; little birds building their nests in the garden; the cry of a newborn baby. Only faith in the Lord can open our eyes and show us the meaning of the nature of life. So it was that day, long ago, when Saint Mungo performed this first miracle with the grace of God.

The Hazel Catkin Holy Flames

With the passing of time, the esteem held between Servanus and the young Mungo grew stronger, and the envy of some of the boys also grew. Some were even plotting to drive the young Mungo from the abbey. It might have been a lonely place to be for Mungo, but the young man accepted his lot, his devotion to the teachings of Jesus more than filling his days.

It was a custom of the pious Servanus to entrust each of the boys, for one week, to light the candles which burned on the altar in the monastery chapel during the celebration of daily mass. This was an important duty, as part of it entailed keeping the fire that burned in the monastery kitchen alight at all times – a task which demanded the nominated boy feed the fire before he retired at night. It was from this fire that the flame was taken and delivered to light the altar candles. Each week Servanus would select one boy who had worked hard in his lessons and, as this was a very great honour to receive, the boys took great pride in performing this task. Wintertime was giving way to springtime when Mungo was given the honour. The cold winds were still whistling through the abbey, so it was most important that the fires should not die out, not only for the lighting of the candles but for the cooking of the meals. The kitchen fire was also the only heating in the abbey.

As he selected Mungo, Servanus told him that it would be the most shameful of things if, through neglect, the fires in the kitchen were allowed to burn out. If this happened the monks would be unable to celebrate the sacred vigils of mass because there would be no flame to light the candles with. Mungo set about diligently carrying out his tasks. Each night he would walk along the draughty corridors of the abbey, go into the kitchen and build up the fires. Then in the mornings he would rise very early, run down to the kitchen, light an ember – making sure not to let it go out – and carry the ember to the chapel, lighting the candles

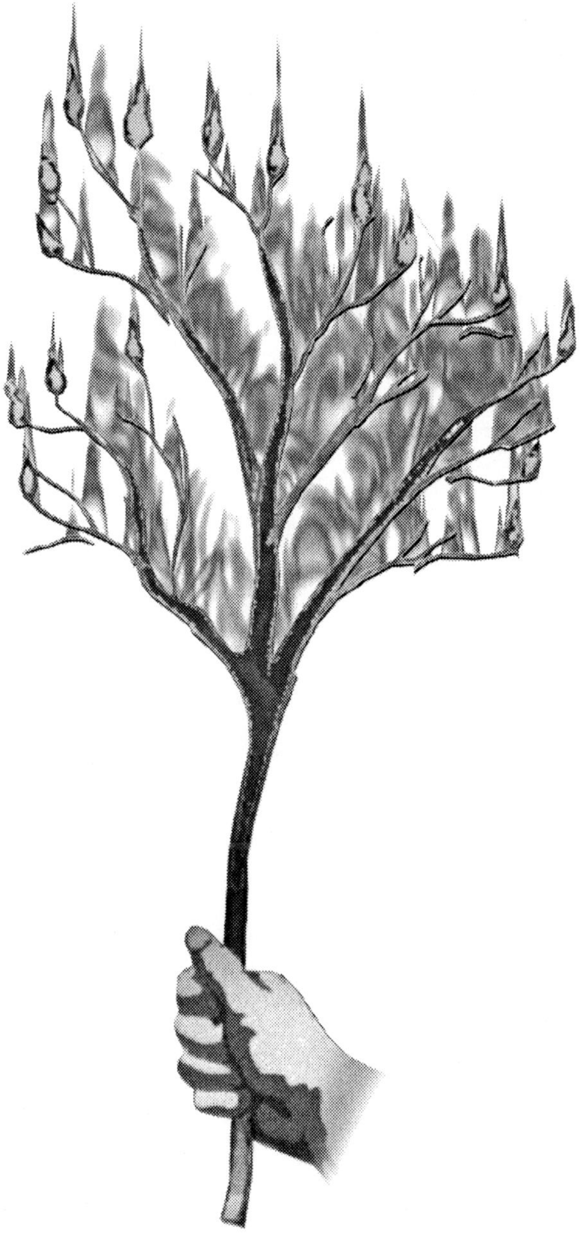

on the altar. Servanus was pleased, and was very loud in his praise of Mungo. Mungo, too, was pleased everything was going along smoothly.

On the eve of the Lord's day, Mungo was especially diligent in his preparations. This night he waited until everyone was in bed before creeping out, so as not to disturb anyone. He threw his bed blanket round his shoulder to keep out the cold and hurried down the long dark corridors of the abbey. Arriving at the kitchen, he made himself busy, carrying the fuel over to the fire and banking it up. When he was satisfied the fire was all right, he warmed himself by the fireside and thanked the Lord. He hoped that it would be a very special mass the next day. He then hurried back along the cold dark corridors to his bed in the boys' dormitory, pleased that he hadn't disturbed the other boys. Once in bed, he promised himself he would rise earlier, allowing more time to prepare everything. As he drifted off to sleep, he was unaware of the movement in the dormitory. His rivals, inflamed by the torches of envy, blinded by jealousy (as is the way of people who envy others who make good of themselves – these people of envy have not the moral fibre to succeed themselves. They will try to prevent and depreciate the good in others, just for their own warped pleasure), waited until he slept, then slipped out of bed and quietly hurried down the corridor to the kitchen.

There, they set about their task of discrediting Mungo. First they removed all the fuel that Mungo had banked up on the fire, then they doused the smouldering embers with water. They extinguished all the fires within the monastery, and the places in the neighbourhood, and then scampered back like thieves in the night, giggling at the deed they had done. Surely this would undo the bond between Servanus and young Mungo, they thought. Quietly they sneaked into their beds, vowing to get up early enough to see Mungo's face when he discovered their deed.

Next morning Mungo was up, even before the first cockcrow. Quietly, he put on his clothes and picked up his sandals, not wanting to wake the other boys. He silently went out of the dormitory and, smiling to himself, hurried down to the kitchen. The sight that met him left him confused and near to tears: the fire was completely cold. *How could this be?* he thought. *I didn't dream that I had banked the fires up.* Mystified, he ran over to the fire, but, hard as he tried to rekindle it, his efforts were all in vain. Mungo was so distraught he didn't know where to turn. He prayed to the Lord for guidance, but none was forthcoming. He prayed again, but still he could not set the fire to light. He didn't know how he would be able to face his master and mentor Servanus again. Just then he heard the scuffling of feet in the corridors. How could he face them now and hear all the boys laughing at him? This was the Lord's day, but with no flame to light the candles they would not be able to carry out the mass with all due solemnity. Thinking of Servanus' last words about the importance of the lighting of the candles, Mungo in his state could not bear to confess.

Gathering his shoulder cover he ran down the corridor, past the friars and boys who were on their way to celebrate mass. On reaching the outer doors he hesitated. *Should I go back and throw myself at the mercy of Servanus?* The humiliation of it all was too much; he opened the door and ran out into the cold morning. Through the courtyard he ran without looking back. He climbed over the surrounding fence and ran as fast as his legs could carry him over the field, only slowing up a little when he reached the woods. Once in the woods, he felt calmness come over him. The air was still and the only sounds he could hear were of the little animals stirring from their slumber. Deeper and deeper he went into the woods until he came to a clearing; here he decided to rest. By this time Mungo had reasoned that it must have been the boys who so disliked him who had in their wicked ways carried out this deed to turn Servanus against him.

Sitting in the clearing, with only the sound of birds whistling, Mungo had time to gather his thoughts. Servanus would be disappointed that he had run away, but he decided that if he was the cause of the wickedness in those boys who were so determined to chase him out, then he would just leave. Then again Servanus had been like a father to him, and was the only kin, apart from his mother, that he had left. She would also have been very worried. What would they think of him if he ran away?

He sat there for what seemed to be an eternity, but it was only minutes. Just as he was pondering what to do, a beam from the morning sunlight spilt through the trees on to the little grassy opening where he was sitting. Mungo stood up and wondered if this might be a sign from God. Animated by faith, he besought the Father of Light to lighten his darkness, by creating a new light, and in a new way preparing a lamp for him, by which he might confuse his enemies who were persecuting him. Lifting his arms up to the heavens, Mungo, with tears in his eyes, prayed to the Lord for forgiveness for all his failings and prayed for the forgiveness of the boys who resented him enough to do this thing. When no answer was forthcoming, in his despair Mungo grabbed a branch from a catkin tree near him and broke it off. The catkins on the branch were in full bloom and shimmering in the sunlight. Looking again to the heavens, he raised his pure hand and traced the sign of the cross upon the branch. Blessing it in the name of the Father, he breathed on it. The pollen spread around in the air, giving a glow around the branch. As he stood there praying, a marvellous and wonderful thing happened: a flame descended from heaven and appeared to dance around the catkin branch. Slowly, the flame settled on the catkins, but it was not like any flame he had seen before. The flames were bright and sent forth rays, spreading out in all directions, turning the darkness to light – but the catkins weren't burning.

The peel of the bells from the monastery, calling the parishioners to morning mass, brought Mungo out of his special dream. He knew then what he had to do. With the branch held high, he ran as fast as he could back through the woods and across the field, jumping over the fence without noticing it was there. He was still holding the catkin branch high as he entered the monastery, hurrying along the corridor. As he passed the torches that were on the wall, they burst into flame, and the light dispelled the darkness. He stopped at the entrance to the chapel; he could hear a lot of voices from inside.

Servanus was already there, along with all the friars and parishioners, and all were looking at the altar and talking among themselves. The boys who had created the problem were huddled together feeling smug. *At last*, they thought, *we've rid ourselves of that pious Mungo*. Then a strange crackling noise was heard coming from the entrance to the chapel. Turning round, Servanus saw Mungo standing in the doorway.

'Mungo, what have you done?' he called. It was only then that he noticed the glowing catkin branch held above Mungo's head.

Mungo, oblivious to all the remarks being said around about him, strode purposefully forward towards the altar of God. He climbed the few steps in front of the altar and stopped. Turning to face the congregation he made the sign of the cross with the catkin branch above their heads. Turning once more to face the altar, and praising the Lord Jesus Christ, one by one he lit all the candles until the bright glow lit up the whole chapel so that the divine office of that day would be celebrated and performed in due season.

The Lord was Mungo's light and his salvation, that he might no longer fear his rivals, because He had judged him and pled his cause against those unjust envious and deceitful boys, that their malice might no more prevail against him.

The whole assembly was struck with awe; they knelt down, amazed at what they were witnessing. When Mungo was done lighting the candles, he turned once again to face the congregation. Holding the catkin branch above his head, he said a prayer of thanksgiving to the Lord, making the sign of the cross with the catkin branch. To their amazement, all that were assembled in the chapel saw the little tongues of flames dance around the branch, then climb up to the top to form one big flame. Slowly the flame died away, leaving the catkin branch as green as if no flame had touched it.

Servanus was the first to react. Going forward to Mungo he threw his arms around him, and with tears in his eyes, he said, 'The Lord above has surely blessed you more than most men. You are truly a chosen son of the Almighty God.' Turning to the whole assembly he said, 'Today, we have witnessed the true love of the Lord that has been bestowed on one he has favoured. Great things will come from this.'

It is said that Servanus ordered some friars to take the catkin branch which had received the blessing from Mungo out into the middle of the field and plant it, and thereafter it began to grow into a tree. Folklore has it that, from that day on, whenever the monks needed to light the fires in the abbey, all they had to do was break a small branch from the catkin tree that was planted in the middle of the field and breath on it to light the fires. Folklore also has it that once the branch grew into a bush, people around the district would, when needed, break even the greenest twig off the catkin bush to light their fires.

From early on in Mungo's life, God had shown many favours to him. Even at a young age it is said Mungo would go around the villages nearby, curing the sick in mind and body. It is also said he performed healing miracles. The people loved him; even then they looked on Mungo as a saint. The legend of Mungo spread further afield, and many more miracles were attributed to his name. When he started going out and about to preach the word of the Lord Jesus he was met with open arms. The Picts, although warrior-like, were also superstitious, so much so that when a saintly man like Mungo came into their midst they were in awe of such a powerful person, and they would listen attentively to his preaching of the word of Jesus. Saint Mungo strengthened the faith in some and converted many others to the Christian faith. Folklore has it that that also was how Mungo was treated even when he was only a young boy. The legend of his deeds would spread out before him and, wherever he travelled, God was always by his side.

The story of the miracle of the catkin branch was first told in the Book *Vita Kentigerni* by Jocelyn, a monk from Furness Abbey. Most recently in 1995 it was adapted in English by I G Capaldi, SJ. This version of this story is mostly my own and follows along the same lines as theirs, with some variations.

The Growing Years of Mungo

Mungo's teenage years were the most important time in his development towards priesthood. It was a time when obedience to the will of God and His teachings could be swayed by the pleasures of life. Some boys who could not take to the monastic life left their calling, but were still better for all the education they had received. Some, though, whose calling was stronger, grew deeper in faith and would one day travel out to spread the gospel of the Lord Jesus Christ to the people in far-off places. In Mungo, the Lord had already mapped out his life ahead. His destiny would take him to places he hadn't even heard of, but for now Mungo obeyed the commands of his sacred order and his mentor, Servanus, by learning from his every word.

All the young students were expected, as were all the monks, to labour in the fields that produced the vegetables for their table. Their normal routine was to rise up early in the morning and, before leaving their cells, lie down prostrate on the cold stone floor, thanking the Lord for all the blessings He had given them and asking Him to be their guide throughout the coming day. Every morning the holy dedication of mass was offered up in the name of the Lord Jesus Christ.

After mass, the whole assembly would retire to the dining hall, which had two long tables stretching to its full length, one on either side. The monks sat on the right-hand side with the novices on the left, all with their backs to the wall. At the far end, in the middle, was situated a raised platform with a lectern. On this lay the Holy Bible, from which, every morning in turn, someone would read text as the assembly ate breakfast. On the end wall behind the lectern hung a cross. This cross was hewn from a solid piece of rock by craftsman, who must have been guided by the Lord, as no mere mortal could have possessed such skill to produce something so beautiful, carried out the carvings.

The meals were generally served by the monks themselves –

no parishioners were allowed into the dining hall during this solemn time – when the breaking of the breakfast bread took place each morning – as this was when they carried out the ancient tradition passed down from the Apostles of commemorating the Last Supper with Christ.

Most of the year, at the start of each day, the food the monks ate was of the simplest kind: bread, cheese and butter. On special occasions, like the celebration of the birth of Jesus, Easter time, or the celebrations of the saints the monks would be allowed to eat meat from pigs and vegetable soup brewed to a broth. To drink they had goat's milk, water and a wine brewed by their own hands from the abundant fruits of the trees. These were all the gifts from the Lord, who in return asked for obedience and honest labour in tending His garden. This the monks did with faithful obedience and hard work to the glory of the Lord. Even in his youth, Mungo understood the reasons for this lifestyle. He had learned from the Bible that even Moses had had to cleanse himself by merging himself into the elements of nature; only in this way would he be close to the Lord.

The celebrations of the Lord's birth in December fell when even on the darkest of days a miraculous light shone to guide the hearts and souls of men to a better life for the glory of the Lord Jesus Christ. The celebration of the first Christmas was very different to what we know today: the emphasis was on the religious aspect of the glorious birth of Our Lord. Mass would be said continuously throughout the night.

Then, after everyone had attended morning mass, the doors of the abbey would be thrown open as a sign that all were welcome into the Lord's house. All the parishioners would be welcomed into the great hall to join in the celebration feast. The local woodsmen supplied the food for the table for the special day and wine and ale would be served from the cellars of the monastery. Celebrations would start a few weeks before Christmas with an old pagan festival called Saturnalias (the planet Saturn was at its brightest in the skies during the month of December). This celebration was incorporated into the Christian faith in the early days. The day before Yuletide was called Wassail Day, when the people drank to one another's health from the Wassail Cup and in

Scotland this custom later moved to become our New Year celebrations.

In those dark days, holy days were the most important days for the fledgling Christians and cherished greatly. On the occasion of Lent, and leading right up to Easter Day, most would fast for days: only a piece of bread and water would be allowed to pass their lips, and only to be taken at night before retiring to bed. When Easter day arrived, the monks would parade around the grounds of the abbey and all through the buildings, sanctifying everything and everyone in the name of the risen Lord. Mungo, like all the other students, helped the monks in their preparations for this great day, which brought a bright new beginning for the strengthening of the faith of all who would hear the word of the Lord and for the giving up of their old ways.

May Day was celebrated in those earliest of days by the lighting of bonfires called Beltane fires. This festival went far back into the dark, dark days when the only masters of religion were the Druids. When Christianity established itself among the people, the apostles of the Lord found it very difficult at first to stop these rituals. Rather than fight them, they educated the people and spread the word that this was in fact the special time of the year dedicated to the Virgin Mary, the mother of our Lord Jesus Christ. Eventually, May Day became the holy day of the Virgin Mother. To this day we still set aside the month of May for devotion to the Holy Mother.

As he grew older, Mungo became more aware of his debt to the Lord and never felt worthy of the faith the Lord placed in him. So, in his teens, he started to do penance for what he considered to be his failings. His bed was a stone slab and his pillow a stone with a hollowed-out part for his head. Of his clothes, it is said that he wore a garment of rough sackcloth near to his skin, under a coat made of goatskin. On top of this, he wore a hooded, long shirt with a tie around his waist. Later on, after he was consecrated into the priesthood, he wore a white alb on top. It is said he never went without a stole to cover his shoulders. The weight of all these clothes was surely a penance on its own. During this period in his life, Mungo started to go to the nearby burn, regardless of the weather, to cleanse himself. At first he would partially remove some clothing, but as he got older he would enter into the burn and submerge himself fully clothed, possibly thinking to himself that walking about all day with damp clothes on would be an additional penance for his unworthiness, and would please the Almighty God. The Lord, looking down on Mungo, heard his penitential prayer and would not let him cause more punishment on himself. With a breath of warm air from the Lord's own mouth, Mungo's clothes, even as he arose from the depth of the water, would be dried as though no water had touched him.

The young Mungo was growing up to be tall in stature. By the time he was nineteen he had reached his full height and was over six feet tall. He was, as it is said, a 'gentle giant'. With all the labour in the fields and the work to extend the monastery to meet the ever-increasing number of students to the monastic service, Mungo's body was becoming as tough and durable as his will to serve the Almighty God. His was a faith that the weaker-minded students were unable to undermine. As hard as they tried, it was to no avail.

Mungo became more his own man and preferred the solitude of the countryside, where he could be closer to God. He would, if not carrying out his duties for Servanus, take himself off into the woods to be alone with nature. The animals, even the wild creatures of the forest, would creep close to be near him as he said his prayers; all night long they would keep vigil over him. Many times in Mungo's life to come, the Lord would guide him through the use of the animals in the forest. It is said the Lord in His wisdom gave Mungo the gift of disarming the people and animals he met by making them feel at ease within themselves.

As the years passed by, with the Lord's help, Mungo's wisdom was called more and more to settle religious questions. Even his mentor, Servanus, who had taught him everything he knew, seeing he had wisdom far beyond his years, would on occasion seek out Mungo for his council. The pupil was now becoming the teacher, and, with this in mind, Servanus, who had such love and faith in Mungo, was leading him on the path to become his successor. For some time, though, the Lord had blinded Servanus to the path Mungo would be destined to take.

In the year in which Mungo was to receive his priesthood, his need for solitude became greater, as if the Lord was preparing him for something special. It was during this time, on one of his excursions into the solitude of the forest, that the Lord used an animal to guide Mungo to the place where he would find a staff that was blessed by the Lord. It happened that Mungo was deep in prayer when a fox came into the clearing where he knelt. The little fox circled Mungo three times before drawing his attention. On seeing the fox, Mungo spoke gently to it.

'What, may I ask, can I do for you, my little friend?'

The fox looked deeply into Mungo's eyes and, with a swish of its tail, turned and ran to the edge of the grove as though beckoning Mungo to follow. Being curious, Mungo followed the fox deep into the forest until he came upon a young tree. The tree had lost all the foliage from its crest, and the top had bent into a crook shape, as though the little tree was crying for the loss of its leaves.

Garlanded around the trunk was a rose bush in full bloom, even though it wasn't the blossoming season. As Mungo approached, a beam of light centred on the little tree. A voice told

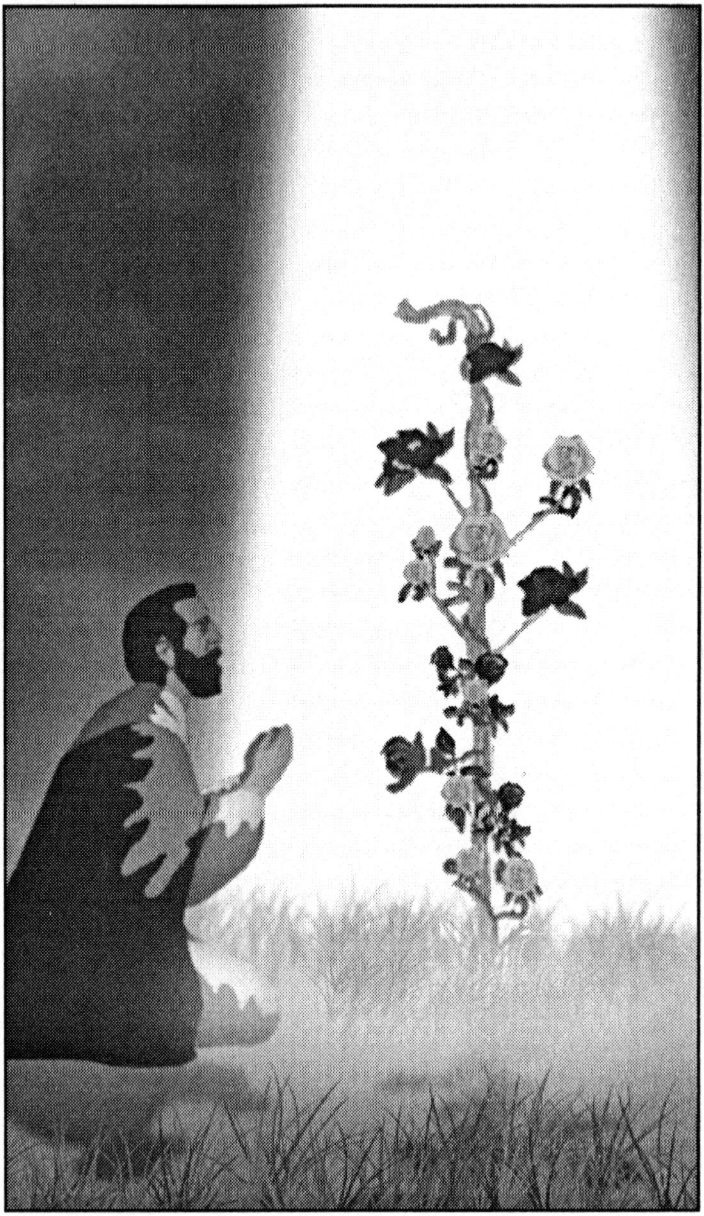

him to cut down the tree, for this would be his staff; no ordinary staff, but one that had been blessed by the Lord Himself. This was the staff that Mungo could trust in with confidence. After Mungo had cut down and prepared his staff, he ran his hands over the full length and found that the Lord had prepared for him a staff of the likeness of the one that Moses had parted the Red Sea with. This would be the staff and rod that would break the bonds of the pagan races, and no sword or weapon would prevail against it.

As Mungo walked back through the wooded area, his little fox companion disappeared back into the forest and, as he passed by, the branches of the trees bowed out of his way, making his path straight. When Mungo returned to the monastery, the monks and students all noticed a difference in him. He had a self-assurance that had earlier been missing. Servanus knew by looking at him that Mungo had been in the presence of the Lord, as the Lord had shown favour on one whom He was best pleased with.

As was the custom in those days, the consecration of new students into the brotherhood took place in the month of May, the month of the Holy Mother, a time of year when the countryside blossoms in all its glory. Like the blossoming of nature, the young students had reached maturity in their faith and were ready to take their place in furthering the blossoming of the holy faith. In the weeks leading up to the holy day, Mungo and the other students went through their final preparations. This would be the most wonderful day of their lives: the Holy Spirit would descend on them and things would never be the same again. Some, with the calling of the Lord, would go out among the people and spread the gospel; others would spend the rest of their days praising the Lord and living a simple religious life. Even a simple life to these monks would break the backs of other mere mortals. To join the Lord Jesus Christ in heaven was what they strove for.

Mungo, more than most, felt the coming of this sanctified day and feared he was unworthy of it, even after all the blessings the Lord had bestowed on him. The Lord looked down on Mungo and, knowing he was like a child about to go out into the strange world with no idea what the Lord had set out for him, calmed his fears and strengthened his resolve to overcome his doubts. During May, the parishioners held festivals that had started life as pagan festivals, but had been incorporated into the Christian calendar of religious festivals.

Mungo was about to reach his twenty-fifth year on this earth, about to blossom out after his consecration into the priesthood. He was ready to take his place, after being tutored for all these years by the Lord through his devoted servant, Servanus.

On the great day when the students were to be consecrated into the priesthood, a procession around the abbey took place. At all corner points of the abbey Mungo, along with the other students, stopped, knelt down and offered up prayers of thanksgiving to the Lord. Awaiting the return of the procession with anticipation, the monks had taken up their places in the chapel – all was in place. The students were still dressed in their normal everyday clothes, and as the procession entered into the chapel the monks began chanting of praises to the Lord. Each student was led to his appointed spot in front of the altar, where he knelt first, then prostrated himself on the floor. Servanus, dressed in a special alb, which was only worn on special occasions like this, stood on the top step in front of the altar. On both sides of him stood two monks of great wisdom and dedication, whose calling was to teach these future priests the skills of converting the people to Christianity. (Sometimes we tend to forget that it was through the skills of these men that the monks and priests were able to spread the holy gospel.)

Each student was called up the steps to the front of the altar, in turn. Here the Holy Spirit descended on them, and Servanus laid his hands on each student in turn, blessing and sanctifying them, and praying that the Lord would guide them from this day on. After all had past through this sacred ritual, the students retired into the sanctuary part of the chapel, where they were given their white albs, a symbol of purity in the eyes of the Lord. Once they had all donned their albs they were led back into the chapel to be finally consecrated into the priesthood of the Lord. In those days, the white alb was normally only worn on special occasions. Mungo, it was said, only ever wore a white alb and it is said that this bequest came down from heaven above.

Nothing has been written about this time in Mungo's life, or how he came by his trusty staff. This story is my own impression of what may have happened as he grew up into manhood.

The Monastery Cook

The saintly Servanus had a certain man, a very old friend, who worked in the kitchen. This man was an important and necessary member of the abbey, and was skilled in his art. He was active and carefully attended to the frequent ministry of preparing all the meals. It came to pass that he was seized by a very serious illness and lay in bed. With the disease increasing and prevailing, he yielded up his breath to the one whom is the breath of all life. Sorrow at his death filled the heart of Servanus, and all the disciples felt the same.

On the day after his burial, all the disciples and servants, the jealous as well as the friendly, came to Servanus. They asked him to summon Mungo through prayer and compel him, by virtue of his obedience to Servanus, to endeavour to raise his cook from the dead. For those who were envious recalled that on the testimony of John of the Apocalypse, the disciples of the Antichrist would send down fire from heaven, and many wizards would, in the eyes of all, do what seemed wonderful things by their wicked arts. But no one of the human race could bring back to life anyone who was really dead, unless he was perfect in holiness like the Lord Jesus Christ.

They persisted, urging Servanus with persuasive words that he, Mungo, should prove his holiness with such a work, and that his merit would be proclaimed for ever if he recalled to life the man who was dead. At first Servanus hesitated to ask Mungo to perform such an unusual deed, but at length, overcome and constrained by the importunity of their wickedness, he talked to Mungo of the matter with gentle words and prayers, but found him reluctant, asserting that he had not the merit for it. Then Servanus adjured him, by the holy and terrible name of the Lord, that he should at least attempt to do what he could, and this he commanded in virtue of holy obedience.

Mungo, fearing adjuration and deeming obedience better and

more pleasing to God than all sacrifices, went to the grave where the Cook had been buried the day before and caused the earth to be dug up and cast out. Then, falling down upon the ground alone, shedding many tears and having his face covered with them, he said, 'Oh Lord Jesus Christ, who is the life and resurrection of your own, who faithfully believe in you. Who kills and makes alive; who brings down to the grave, and brings up. To whom life and death are servants, who did raise up Lazarus, when he had been dead four days, raise again this holy man who is dead, that your holy name will be glorified above all things, blessed for ever'. Then a thing exceedingly astonishing happened. While Mungo poured forth many prayers, the dead man, prostrate in the dust, straight away rose again from the dead, and came forth, though bound in grave cloths. He wearily rose from death, as the other rose from prayer, and along with him and a great crowd following him, he proceeded safe and active, first to the church to give thanks to God, and then by the command of Mungo to his office in the kitchen, everyone applauding the miracle and praising God. But he who was raised from the dead afterwards described the punishments of the wicked, and the joys of the righteous which he saw, and in so doing turned many away from evil to good.

Being urged by many, he likewise unfolded the manner of his resuscitation. He asserted that he was torn from human things with unspeakable pain and led before the tribunal of the terrible Judge, and that there he saw many who, on receiving their sentence, were cast into hell, others destined to Purgatory, and some raised to Eternal Joy. And when he tremblingly expected his own sentence, he heard that he was the man for whom Mungo was praying. And the same cook, preferring sacred religion in habit and in act, lived for another seven years. When he was buried there was engraved on the lid of the coffin how he was raised from the dead by Saint Mungo, that by all who see, or shall see it in time to come, the wonderful God may be glorified in his saint. The grave of the Cook could be seen for many a long year in the grounds of Culross Abbey.

This story about the miracle of the dead cook raised by Saint Mungo is dedicated to an elderly lady who wrote it many years ago. She came from High Valleyfield, and sadly passed away a few years ago. I have altered it slightly to bring it more in line with my own stories.

Culross Abbey ruins and church. The ruins pictured here were built on top of the former abbey and added to. These ruins date back to around AD 1200. The church below is a younger building built on top of the old ruins.

*The interior of Culross Abbey.
On the stained-glass windows behind the altar can be
seen the depictions of Saint Mungo and Saint Serf (Severanus).*

The Journey begins

When Mungo had been visited by the angel a second time, the message was clear: those around him were sorely testing his trust in the Lord, and especially his obedience to Servanus. It was his mentor who had pushed Mungo's faith in the Lord to the limit, by insisting that he should ask the Lord to grant him a miracle. The cook had been restored to life, but at a cost to himself.

In the year AD 543, the angel told him that his time in Culross was at an end, and the Lord had a far greater mission for him. He was to leave all his friends, and his teacher, his beloved Servanus, and sneak away without saying goodbye. So, like a shadow in the night, he gathered his staff and his prayer book and, with only the clothes he wore, silently left. As he left the abbey that had been his home since his birth, a pang of sadness came over him and he felt guilty. Once he was outside the walls of the abbey, he knelt down and asked the Lord to forgive his guilt and to bless all he had left behind. He started down the steep brae.

'My trust is in Lord for He is good. He will provide for me,' he sang as he walked into the night. Down the rickety path he travelled until he reached the river.

Before continuing his mission he made one more stop, visiting the spot by the river's edge where he had been born. Here he knelt down and prayed.

'Dear Lord, I thank You for blessing me and for the many gifts You have bestowed on me, for all the dear friends I have known. Please Lord, forgive those who know not Your designs for me, give me the strength to carry out Your will. I am and will always be Your humble servant.'

Pausing for a moment, then leaning on his staff, he slowly stood up and took one last look at the place. He made the sign of the cross, blessing the spot where he had been born. Without looking back, he strode purposely into the night, travelling along the side of the River Forth and heading in a westerly direction, which was the way the angel had said he should go. It was still dark, with a clear, starry sky, and he was able to follow the river for the most part. Only when it was impassably marshy did he move into the forest. The stars, shining through the treetops, brightened the darkness. Onward he travelled, stopping for a rest every few miles, singing psalms and praying. As he walked, the praise of the Lord was never far from his lips, and he knew he was not alone on this journey, for he could feel the hand of God guiding his every footstep.

The next day he found his way back to the river and followed it. He could see the river was getting narrower and narrower as he reached a point called Cinncardden (Kincardine).[1] Here the forest was right down to the river edge. So he knelt down and asked the Lord for guidance. From here, he was to travel inland through the forest. The forests in those days were full of Caledonian bears, wild boar and wild cats – all kinds of danger lurked behind every bush. Fearlessly he set out into the forest, sometimes using his staff to clear a path, and eventually he came to a clearing near Kilbagie. It was hear he met an old monk who was living like a hermit. The old man had heard about Mungo's miracles and wasn't surprised to see him; it had been revealed to him in his sleep that the servant of God would pass his way.

Mungo stayed awhile and listened to the old hermit's stories of trials and failures. The hermit had for some time been trying to Christianise the heathen Pict tribes of the Mannan area without success. Mungo learned that the Roman soldiers had retreated from their outpost at Athluath.[2] When the Romans departed from their outpost the Picts moved back in to take full control of the area and enforce their old barbaric ways. Once he had heard all about the trials of his friend, Mungo decided to confront the chief of this tribe, who, it was said, still sometimes gave human sacrifices to his god, Manua, a sea god worshipped by the Druids.

Mungo stayed with his friend the rest of that day. They sang psalms and prayed, as was the custom of the monks. Mungo also attended to the old man's spiritual needs.

---

[1] Cinncardden, meaning 'at the head of the wood'. Place names taken from George Mackay, *Scottish Place Names*, Lomond, 2000.

[2] Alloa, meaning 'swift ford'. This was noted by the Roman Army, as the first point the forth could be crossed at low tide; a burial site stands at Mars Hill, also the probable remains of a Roman outpost.

Ruin of Saint Mungo's Chapel, built around the year 1503 by the Archbishop Blackadder, the then archbishop of Glasgow. On this spot it is said that Saint Thenew gave birth to Saint Mungo around AD 517. It is situated on the left-hand side of the A985 to Toryburn road, 150 yards east of Culross.

Next morning Mungo was up before the first cockcrow. After saying his morning prayers, he gathered some wild berries and poured the dew off the tops of leaves into a cup. In the small stream nearby, he cleansed himself. The water was very cold, but to Mungo this was a penance which he accepted. He shared his bounty with his old friend. He knew it was time he must be on his way, but before he said his farewell, he knelt down to pray and asked the Lord to guide his tongue when he met his pagan foes. He embraced his old hermit friend and, with a wave, departed.

Meanwhile, back in Culross, Servanus was starting to worry about his beloved student. Mungo had from time to time gone into the woods on his own for a day or two before, but this was different – Servanus had not been privy to the Lord's plans for Mungo. Mungo had never missed morning adoration twice in a row before. Servanus, who was getting on in years, had harboured the thought that one day Mungo would take over as abbot when he himself had passed on to join the Lord in heaven. Worried, he sent out some students to search for Mungo. All returned later, with no sightings. Servanus then sent some of the friars in different directions to look further afield. Gathering everyone together, they went into the chapel to pray for Mungo's safe return.

Mungo entered the woods, walking in a westerly direction. The birds in the trees were singing their morning prayers to the Lord, and this gave Mungo heart to face the task before him. After a while he noticed smoke above the treetops, and he knew this would be some sort of settlement. He strode out in that direction, as he got nearer he was surprised by the movement up ahead – figures moving between the trees. Suddenly some men jumped out to bar his path. Undaunted, Mungo kept walking on until he was challenged.

These were the Picts who his old friend had told him about. The warriors stood resplendent in their body paint, looking menacingly at Mungo. Mungo advanced right up to the warriors and looked them in the eyes; what they saw made them step back, for this was no ordinary man. No man before had been able to look into their eyes, even into their very soul, like he did.

Mungo raised his hand, showing the palm, and said, 'Peace be with you.' To men of war this was a strange greeting, and one that confused their hearts.

The first impression is, as they say, the best one, and it was for the first meeting for Mungo and the Pict tribe. The warriors were in disarray; they were lost as to the action they should take.

Sensing this, Mungo said to them, 'Do not be afraid, the one Almighty God has sent me to enlighten your people.'

Who can this man be? they thought. *Who dares to face us with only a book as a shield and a wooden staff for a weapon?*

They were about to find out that the word of God was indeed mightier than the sword. The warriors looked at one another and, as if of one mind, they turned and retreated, melting back to the forest from whence they came.

Mungo decided to stay at that spot in the woods. Here he knelt down and read some passages from his prayer book, knowing the warriors would return. Rather than impose himself on them, he thought it would be better for them to return of their own accord. A period of time passed, and Mungo, still on his knees praying, became aware that many eyes were watching him from behind the trees. He turned the pages of his prayer book and read aloud, his voice like a gentle breeze on a warm day, but with a melodious sound. Before long some of the native people, both men and women, came out of the woods. Seeing that they were in no danger, they edged closer. Gradually some moved even closer and sat down. They had never heard such wonderful words; if they had looked up they would have seen that even the angels in heaven had stopped to listen.

All afternoon Mungo read and preached to them, telling them how God loved them so much that his only son Jesus Christ had died on a cross to pay for all their sins, and how he raised himself up from the dead, and much more. They were like little children, heeding his every word. Seeing it would soon be night, he told them to go home and think of all that he had preached to them. Reluctantly, they agreed, but not before he had promised he would preach to them again. He said to them, 'Tomorrow, at sunrise, I will stand in the middle of your hamlet and greet you with blessings in the name of our Lord Jesus Christ'.

These people were part of the Horestii nation that stretched from parts of Strathclyde right across Fife including Clackmannanshire. They had a reputation for being fearless fighters and in past history had been great adversaries of the Roman legions, or any other foreigner who tried to change their ideology. Even in Saint Mungo's time they were still a very distrustful, barbaric race. Knowing this, Mungo knew he could not show fear, as this would be taken as a sign of weakness. That night he prayed to the Lord to give him a sign, a sign that they would surely know that He had sent this unworthy servant to proclaim the word of Jesus about the Father, the Son and the Holy Spirit.

Very early next morning, before the sun rose, Mungo was already approaching the hamlet called Mannan (Clackmannan). Two guards were guarding the outer perimeter defence wall, but as Mungo walked right up to, and passed by them, he noticed the Lord had made them sleep. Entering the main dwelling enclosure area, all was still except for some dogs that were tied up. They looked at this dark shadowy figure who stood in their midst but did not bark.

He found that the huts were clustered in a circle around a huge rock, which would have been where the Druids practised their ceremonial rites. Situated to one side was a large hut with deer antlers along the top; this building was the only one with a torch burning, and Mungo knew it must be the chief's dwelling. Silently, he walked up to the central edifice. Servanus had taught him that these rocks were probably used as an altar for human sacrifice. He held his hands over the rocks and, praying to the Lord, cleansed them by making the sign of the cross. He then climbed up on top and stood with his arms raised to the heavens, his prayer book in one hand and his staff in the other. Lifting his eyes to the heavens, he said, 'Lord, if it is Your will to grant this lowly servant a sign that these children may see and understand Your mercy, please let it be.'

Mungo waited until the sun was just about to rise above the horizon, then brought his staff down on to the rock with such force that the noise of it was like a clap of very loud thunder, and the ground shook beneath the hamlet. The dogs started to bark and the people tumbled out of their dwellings in disarray, wondering what catastrophe had befallen them. Once they cleared the sleep from their eyes, they saw the dark shadow of Mungo suddenly glow with light from the morning sun rays. Afraid, they cowered back, but Mungo said, 'Peace and the blessings of the Almighty Lord Jesus Christ be with you all.'

Most of those who had heard him speak the day before remembered his promise and dropped to their knees. The chief, though, had not heard of Mungo. He had rushed out of his abode at the noise as if for war. Sword in hand, he approached Mungo, but when he tried to lift his sword to strike he found he had not the strength and stopped in his track. Bewildered by this affliction, he started to curse Mungo but the words would not come out. His thoughts were in confusion. Mungo stepped down from the rock and went up to the chief.

Seeing the bewilderment in his eyes, Mungo said to him, 'Be not afraid. I am only a humble servant of the Lord Jesus Christ, who is the one true God. He has sent me in His name to teach you. I have not come to spill blood but to teach you the way to salvation.'

At this, calm came over the chief. Aggression was no longer in his thoughts. His people were astounded at what they had seen.

Mungo spent the next few days sampling their hospitality, reading text from the letters of the Apostles and teaching them to say the Lord's Prayer. Even the Druids listened, because Mungo did not condemn them but pointed out that the Almighty God had created everything. The news of this great prophet preacher spread out to all the smaller communities, and more and more native people turned up to hear him tell the holy stories. Mungo won over the Druids and Christianised the tribes of that area.

The call came for Mungo from a small scattering of rude abodes called Athluath in a very fertile area situated on both sides of the little burn called the Broth (Brothy burn). The little hamlet had been growing since the Roman Army's occupation of Mars Hill, but it would be changed for ever when Mungo set foot on its soil. The journey from the hamlet of Mannan to Athluath was only a mere one and half miles.

When Mungo reached the hillock overlooking the small hamlet, the view that met him made him gasp at the beauty the Lord had created there. Looking down, Mungo saw that this was indeed a fine place to establish a church. From where he stood, he could see over all the lands right up to the mountains in the north and to the River Forth in the south. This was a very fertile place, with abundant game in the forest and wheat in the fields. Mungo decided to make that spot his resting place, so that he would be able to preach from above an audience. (This spot on the hillock would be for ever a holy place, and in later years would be the place where a battle against the Saxon invaders took place. A stone cross, the Pillar Stone of Broth, still marks the place known as Hawkhill.) How long Mungo stayed we can only guess, but long enough to Christianise the whole area. In order for Mungo to leave a lasting impression on the local people as he has, he must have carried out many marvellous things and possibly a miracle. A church in the hearts of the people was established, but not built of brick or mortar.

Before long, Mungo felt the call from the Lord to carry on with his mission grow stronger. Word came to Mungo that Servanus, in company with his monks, was on the way to speak to him. The night before, an angel appeared to Mungo and told him he must not let this happen, as the Lord's work must come before all else. Mungo made preparations to leave the next day, before Servanus arrived. While staying around the area of Athluath, Mungo may have learned that there was a ford over the River Forth that could be crossed at low tide.[1]

With this in mind, early the next morning Mungo preached to the people, saying, 'I am leaving you today but be not afraid, as I am only the first messenger. Others will follow and help you grow in love for the Lord Jesus Christ. Cast out these pagan gods and follow Jesus Christ, the one true God, my children! Great rewards await you in heaven, so be faithful and follow his Commandments, or damnation will be wrought on you, if you should return to your old ways.'

---

[1] This may be why the Roman army established an outpost here. Athluath, or Alloa, means 'swift ford'. At low tide the river is so shallow that only a narrow swift flowing stream of about fifteen feet or more could easily be crossed over. Fifteen hundred years ago the Forth may have been shallower than it is today.

Mungo picked up his earthly belongings and started down the hill towards the river. It was late afternoon by this time and there was a great number of the village people following behind. At the river's edge he offered up a prayer to the Lord for having made the river tide go out so that he could cross. Turning to say his farewells to his followers, and noticing in the distance his old friend Servanus coming down the hill with his monks, with a quick farewell he turned and crossed over the river dry-shod. When he reached the other side, he prayed to the Lord to take away the burden of having to say farewell to his old friend and mentor, and to give him the will to stop Servanus following him. Lifting both arms up to heaven he said, 'Lord in all Your magnificence, give a sign of Your glory, that Your name will for ever be blessed by the peoples of this place, and let my old friend Servanus see your will be done.'

Just then the clouds rolled in and it grew very dark; the birds in the air and the animals on the earth took refuge, as though forewarned by God. From the other bank, Servanus called out to Mungo to return, but the wind howled so loudly that it blotted out all sound. As Servanus and his followers, along with the people, stood wondering what was happening, to their amazement they saw the river come rushing back in, so much so that the water splashed over the banks, making it impossible for Servanus to follow Mungo.

Servanus looked up to heaven with tears in his eyes. 'Lord,' he said, 'You truly are in all things we do, in all we are and in all we must be. You have sent us a sign, such a glorious sign that Your name through Mungo will for ever be on the lips and in the hearts of all men who are to follow from this day on.'

Looking at the people who had assembled, he said to them, 'Today you are the witnesses of the greatness of the Lord. From this day on we will dedicate this land to our beloved Mungo in the glory of the Lord, for he is beloved by God above all men. To help you complete your conversion to the holy Christian faith, I will leave some of my followers to continue the word Mungo has taught you.'

Mungo, standing on the river edge called out, 'My old friend, do not fret about me, for the Lord in His wisdom has greater things for me to accomplish. My thoughts and prayers will always be of you.' With a final wave of his hand, he turned, and, singing the praises of the Lord Jesus and the Holy Mother, he went forth. Their eyes would never meet again in this life.

Servanus, weary of old age and tired from his journey, rested awhile before returning back to his refuge at Culross. After arranging for one of his monks to stay and carry on the work Mungo had started, he took his leave. With the rest of his companions he returned back to the abbey at Culross. Every day thereafter when in the garden he would give praise to the Lord for having chosen him for the privileged task of educating Mungo, who was truly a saint and a chosen son of the Lord. Servanus lived only a few more years. His body was interred in a crypt under the old abbey church. A Celtic cross on the wall of the ruin abbey, it is said, marks the spot where he is buried. Today a new church stands on the same spot and is dedicated to Saint Serf (Servanus); he is also the patron saint of Culross.

In the Rev. Crouther Gordon's book, *A Short History of Alloa*, he says that nothing is known about the Alloa area until Saint Mungo passed through on his way to Glasgow around AD 540. He also goes on to say that the name of Christ was probably known in this area before the end of that century, but in his book *A History of Clackmannan*, he states that it was Saint Serf who Christianised this area around AD 650. This conflict of dates may be because there were two people called Servanus: one who was the teacher of Saint Mungo and another one who followed later; the later Servanus went on to become Saint Serf. The Rev. James Cooper, DD, Professor of Ecclesiastical History, Glasgow University, writing about the *Three Fathers of the Faith in Scotland*, puts Saint Mungo first in this area for Christianising the people. I can only assume Saint Mungo evangelised the people on his way to Glasgow. The late Rev. A Bryson, in his story, 'Alloa and Tullibody',[2] states:

> Alloa and the surrounding district was evangelised by Saint Mungo, a native of Culross, pupil of Saint Serf. In early times

---

[2] From L Maclean Watt [ed], *Alloa and Tullibody*, Alloa, 1902.

there was a shrine dedicated to him, which was the chapel for the feudal lords and inhabitants of the clachan that by and by grew into the ancient barony of Alloway.

From these sources we can deduce that Saint Mungo spent some time in this area preaching.

Because of the lack of historical evidence, most early historians in the time after Jocelyn's death accepted the original version of the crossing of the Forth in Jocelyn's *Vita Kentigerni*. Not being a learned academic, I can approach this miracle from a different angle. There is no mention in any of my research of Saint Mungo ever being near the Stirling area, which is a further seven miles west of Alloa, even though Stirling was in existence around that time and a Roman road passed nearby. Also some historians place the Roman army under the leadership of Agricola, as crossing over the Forth near Alloa. The Roman outpost having been found on Mars Hill; the meaning of the Alloa name 'swift ford'; the dedication of a church going back to before historical records began; the fact that Carnock is just over the other side of the River Forth and is on the direct route to Glasgow – all these put together have led me to only one conclusion: that this is the first point in the river near Alloa where Saint Mungo would have crossed over.

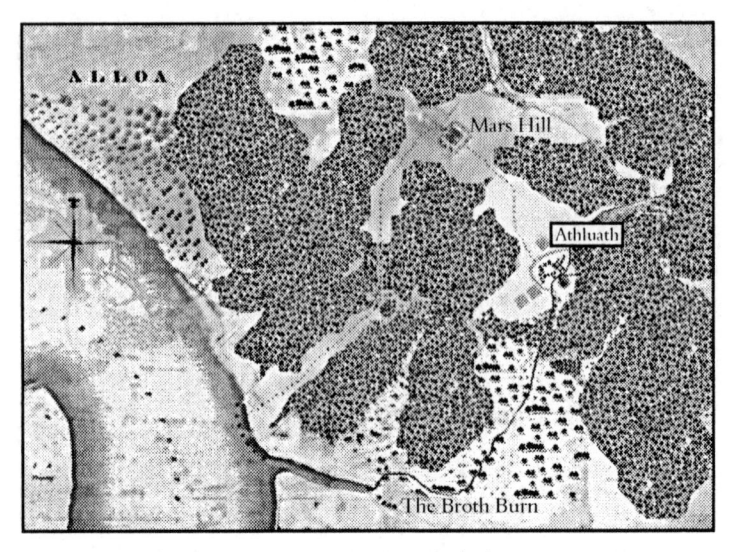

Athluath (Alloa) area as it may have looked around AD 500. 1825 map digitally altered by kind permission of National Map Library and Museum of Scotland

Two churches are dedicated to Saint Mungo in Alloa. The Saint Mungo's Church of Scotland parish church. The old Catholic Church in Clackmannan Road was outgrown and the present Saint Mungo's Catholic Church (below), was built around 1960 in Mar Street.

The remains of the old church, which was dedicated to Mungo, stand on the same spot where the old feudal church stood in Kirkgate Cemetery

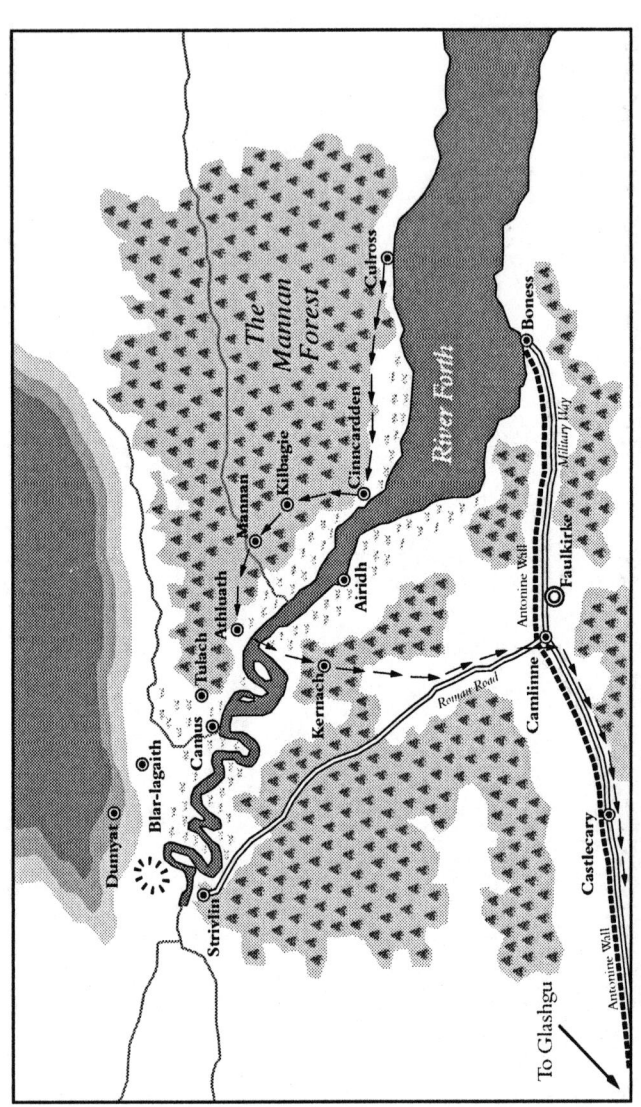

Clackmannanshire around AD 500, the area Mungo travelled through on his journey to Glashgu with Saint Fergus. 'Strivlin' is an older name for Stirling.

Mungo's Journey with Saint Fergus

Turning away from the river, Mungo followed a little path which headed inland. The terrain was much gentler here. He walked along the path for half a mile before it disappeared into a forest. It was late afternoon and starting to get dark, and it was getting near time for Mungo to say his evening psalms, so he decided he would take only a few more steps before stopping.

He had gone a short distance into the forest to a place known as Kernach (Carnock), when he heard music in the distance, and making his way towards the sounds he came into a clearing. Over to one side of the clearing stood a round dwelling place that was fashioned out of tree branches bent over and joined at the top. Smaller branches were entwined around the side in tight formation, with some animal skins stretched and stitched over the framework. In the dim light, Mungo could make out two bullocks grazing at the far side of the clearing. As he got nearer to the abode he could make out the squat figure of an old man sitting near a small fire. His back was to Mungo, who could hear him singing the praises of the Lord, and so he approached.

In a calming voice he said, 'Peace be with you, and may the Lord's blessings be upon you.'

At this the old man wearily turned and tried to stand up, but he was very old and not long for this world. Mungo saw this and rushed to his side, saying, 'The providence of the Lord has surely this day sent me this way. In His wisdom He has guided me to this place to take care of you. It is His will that I stay and pray with you, until you join Him on High who is the breath of all life.'

The old man finally managed to stand up, albeit very shakily. Turning to face Mungo he said, 'I have prayed a long time to the Lord that He would send to me the one He has chosen to carry His word to the nations. Praised is His name for this great gift He has given me, that I should see with these old eyes the

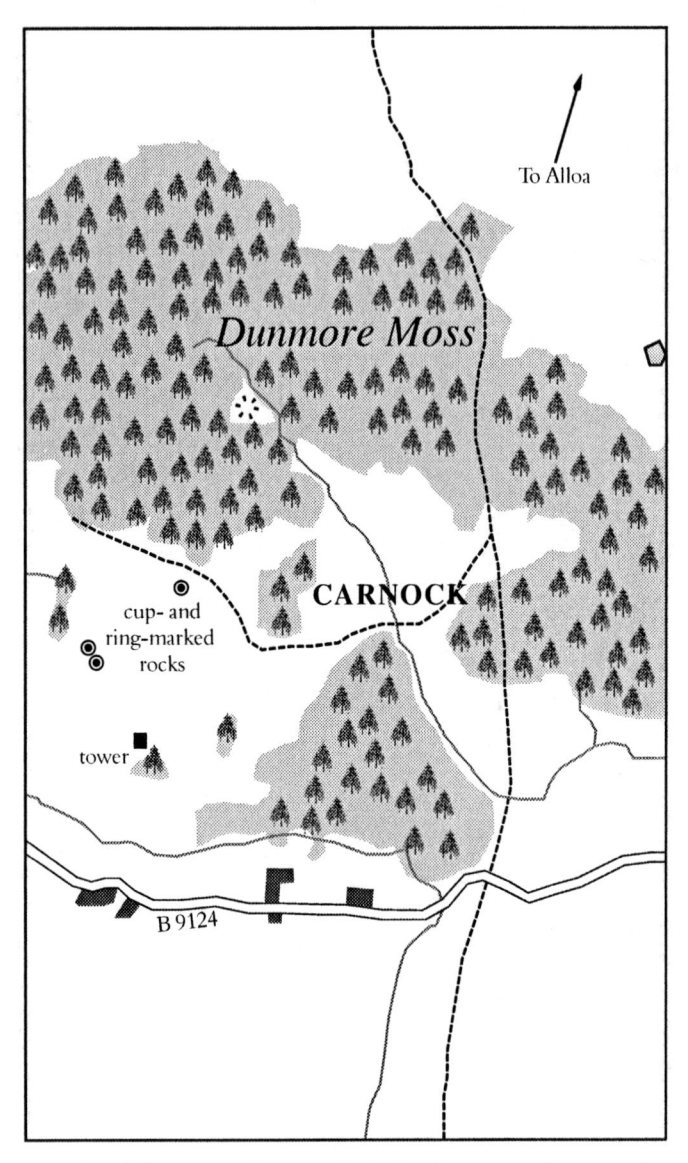

Carnock and the surrounding area, including the cup- and ring-marked rocks. These date back to ancient time and a settlement may have been there at the time Saint Mungo passed this way.

beloved one chosen by the Almighty Lord Jesus Christ. My soul rejoices at this meeting.'

Laying down his staff, Mungo opened his arms and wrapped them around the old man, comforting him. It gave the older man a warm feeling, taking him back to his childhood days when his own mother would comfort him on a cold night, just as the Holy Virgin Mother Mary had done on that cold winter's night when the Light of the World, the baby Jesus, was born.

Mungo broke the silence and said, 'I will tend to your needs as you so wish.' With tears in his eyes the old man went on to tell Mungo his confessions and to speak of his fear that he might die there alone, until one night a messenger in a dream told him of the great saint who would pass his way.

The two of them sat by the fire and shared what little food they had. The old man told Mungo his name was Fergus and his dying wish was that his body be placed on a cart and harnessed to two bullocks. They, in turn, were to be given their free will to travel in whatever direction they pleased; his wish was also that he be buried at the spot where the bullocks came to rest. Mungo sat by his side for the rest of the night, praying and singing psalms.

Fergus died early the next morning, peacefully, in the arms of Mungo, blessed and anointed by the breath of the Holy Spirit. Mungo wrapped his body in the clothes he had worn and covered him with the animal skins that had been his bed, and then placed him on the cart. Fetching the two bullocks, Mungo tied them to the cart.

The early morning had a touch of frost in the air. Mungo was used to submerging himself in the burns of the places he stopped in, and it was no different this morning. After saying his morning prayers he went to the little burn nearby; standing in the middle of it, he raised his hand and his eyes to the heavens, asking the Lord for forgiveness for not having arriving sooner to help old Fergus.

He said, 'Lord, forgive this unworthy sinner for his sins and accept the soul of one who has praised Your name with every word and deed.' He then sank slowly until he was fully submerged; it was as though Mungo was washing away his sins in baptism.

When he emerged from the water, as folklore would have it, Mungo was cleansed but as dry as he had been before going in. His next chore was to send on its way the cart pulled by the two bullocks, which carried the body of Saint Fergus. The bullocks started off in a direction that was familiar to their habit; this direction would take them through the forest. A little further on they turned on to the old Roman road that ran from Callender in the north, to the old fortification of Camelon, built on top of what was to be known as the Antonine Wall. It had once been the main fortification of the mighty Roman legions, but that was over 250 years earlier.

Over the years, Camelon fell into decline and Falkirk is now the dominant town of the area, but in Mungo's time, Camelon was a very important crossroad, being an important market town. During their time the Roman Army built a communication road running along the south side of the Antonine Wall; this they called the Military Way. In its day, this road was one of the main westward routes. Mungo followed the cart pulled by the two bullocks, not knowing where it would lead him. But his faith had taught him that the Lord would let him know his destination in due time.

Passing by Camelon and beyond the wall the bullocks trundled on without a break in their stride. Mungo was a very fit man and felt no need for a rest. Praying as he walked, he kept pace with the cart and marvelled at the beauty of the land before him. The terrain was a little gentler now; after a while the bullocks paused to drink water and eat some grass. All that day Mungo followed the cart, which was still heading west the Military Way. Every now and then he would pass some other old fortifications, which had long since fallen into disrepair. Small villages had sprung up near these old forts, such as Castlecary, Croy Hill, Twechar and Kirkintilloch.

It was near this point that the bullocks turned south at a place known to the locals today as Glasgow Bridge. The land ran gentle down from here and the bullocks could feel their burden getting a lot easier. Mungo could see in the distance a river stretching as far as the eye could see – this was the Rive Clyde; his journey was near its end. The two bullocks, still carrying out their honoured task of conveying the body of Saint Fergus to its resting place, continued down the gravel tracks until they gently stopped at a place known then as Cathures. It was here that a cemetery had been ordained and consecrated by Saint Ninian years before. Mungo, without doubting the Lord's wisdom, knew that this was the place he was ordained to establish a church. The land was very fertile and a little burn called the Molendinar Burn flowed through the valley; this was indeed a place of holiness and tranquillity. Led by these two bullocks to this place that was first chosen by the Lord when Saint Ninian long before consecrated the ground, Mungo knew from that moment that he had come home.

Before resting, Mungo set about preparing the spot he had chosen for the burial of the sacred body of Fergus. Singing psalms, he worked until he was satisfied that he had prepared a grave fit to receive the body of a saint. He then interred Saint Fergus, entrusting him to the keeping of the one who is most high. It is said in folklore that Saint Fergus was the first to be buried there in this hallowed ground, and legend has it that from that day on, whoever trod the ground where Saint Fergus was buried, would suffer the dire consequences for it within the year. This place chosen by the Lord was the place destined to be to be the rebirth of Christianity. So ended the tale of a man called Fergus from Carnock.

Even today, off the Blackadder Aisle, in Glasgow Cathedral, above the entrance to the vault, can be seen a depiction of the holy man, Saint Fergus, lying on the cart on which he was conveyed to his resting place.

Dear Green Place, Glashgu

Glashgu, 'Dear Green Place', was the name Mungo gave to the area of this wonderful land of natural beauty. It was here he set to work clearing the land so that he could establish his church. Mungo was not the kind of man to be put off by hard work; this had always been his way, even in his younger days when he had worked the land of Culross Abbey. Each day he would toil until sunset, then, before having food (consisting of rough bread made from wild wheat to eat and water to drink – Mungo never let ale touch his lips), he would kneel down to thank the Lord for giving him the strength to carry out his task.

He worked alone for days, but he had a feeling he was being observed. His feelings had not deceived him. Some local peasants had watched him, and had seen him bury Saint Fergus's body. They observed with wonder that he sang psalms to the Lord as he worked.

Some had heard of this one Almighty God years before, but had strayed back to their old pagan ways. They were impressed by the dedication of this holy man who worked alone all day, non-stop, without fear. Gaining courage, some ventured forward to find out why he was there.

Seeing them approach, Mungo stopped and said, 'Peace of the Almighty Lord Jesus Christ be with you. Fear no more, your dark days are over, as I have been sent by the Lord who is the one true God in answer to your prayers. He has sent me to establish His church here so that your souls may be saved.'

One man, who looked like the elder of the group, approached and asked, 'When did we ask for your God to come here? We have our own gods whom we pray to.'

With a gesture of his hand, Mungo produced his Bible, which even when working in the fields he always carried under his white alb.

Opening up the book, he quoted in a very loud voice from its pages, 'You shalt not worship false gods or false idols before me, saith the Lord. You shalt not speak the Lord's name in the same breath as these idols.'

The elder was taken aback, so much so that he fell to his knees and asked for forgiveness. Mungo lifted the elder up and told him he was forgiven, saying that they were as little children who did not know any better.

'I will teach you all about the teachings of the Lord Jesus and His holy mother, Mary, in the days to come,' he said. 'But for now the Lord asks for labourers to help me build a house for him. Those who do this will reap great rewards from Him who is the life of all things.' This was how Mungo may have made his first conversions on this hallowed ground.

Each day, more and more peasants appeared and were won over by the saintly man. Many hands, they say, make light work, and this was the case in the early days of Mungo's vocation, as he turned the hearts of the heathen people back to the one God who is the life of the world. Many willing workers came to hear the teachings of Jesus from Mungo, their reward was the building of a church where Mungo would be able to start preparing future disciples to spread the word of Jesus. His first church was built entirely of wood from the nearby forest; trees were felled and, in the fashion of the time, they were split and dragged to the place where Mungo had consecrated a piece of land a stone's throw from the Molendinar Burn. As the weeks went by, the church began to take shape, a church so magnificent that even the people were amazed at what they had built. The dimensions and style have unfortunately long since been lost in the fog of time.

During their rest periods, Mungo would teach his followers all about Jesus. Some of the older people remembered a time years before when another certain saintly man by the name of Ninian had preached about this same Jesus, and had converted them to Christianity. That was long ago, but their faith had been weak and hadn't stood the passage of time – in the years before Mungo arrived they had strayed back to paganism. This time the seeds that were sown years before would burst forth with a new understanding of the word of Jesus.

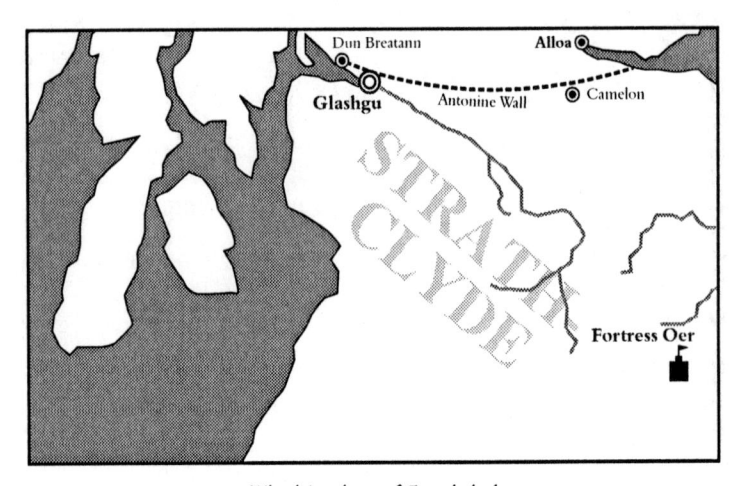

The kingdom of Strathclyde

'Ystrat Clud' (Strathclyde) in those days was called Rheged. The kingdom stretched from the Clach nam Breaton, the stone of Britons, under the shadow of Ben Lomond, in Argyle in the north, all the way down to another marker (Rere Cross, in the Stainmore Pass near Penrith) in the south that is known as Cumbria today. The kingdom of Cambria was divided into clan areas, known by the name of the head of the family, but two families were more ambitious than the rest. The king of the Britons, Elidyr the Handsome, whose stronghold was on Dunbarton Rock (Dun Breatann), was of a mind to have the whole of Cambria Christianised. The other, a pagan king called Morken the Accursed, had rejected the Christian faith in the past and had sworn to destroy anyone who followed this faith. These two opposing kings fought constant battles for supremacy. Elidyr, the king of the Britons, had prayed long to the Lord to send a saint who would sway and convert the subjects of these lands, to cast out their pagan ways and embrace the teachings of the Lord Jesus Christ.

With no steadying religious influences, power had swung back and forth for many years. This was the land that the Lord, having heard the pleas of the good King of the Britons, had commanded Mungo to come to and spread His word. The task before Mungo was formidable, but his faith never wavered for a moment. In the early days, Mungo laboured long and hard to complete his church and to baptise the people who would hear the Word. For some it was only to regenerate their dormant faith; others needed more persuasion, but gradually Mungo could see the fruits of his labour appear in both building and faith.

Soon word reached Elidyr in his fortification near Dumbarton of the wonderful regeneration of the faith that was taking place in his kingdom. He sent messengers to find out just who was the cause of this upsurge of faith. The messengers, on arriving at the ground consecrated by Mungo, were warmly welcomed by Mungo's followers and led to meet their pastor. The messengers were surprised when they were lead across a ploughed field to meet a man who was still working the ground.

Surely this can't be their leader? they thought. *Not this man who gets his hands dirty with manual work.* But the greeting they received from Mungo lit their hearts; all at once their souls were lifted up as if a great cloud had been removed. Recognising that the greatness of the Lord was with this man, they dropped to their knees before Mungo, asking for his blessing and conveying the delight their king and master would have now that his prayers had been answered. They spent some time listening to Mungo, and, after a while, he told them to return to their good king with his blessings and told them that one day soon he would visit him at Elidyr's dwelling place.

The labourers who had come to help Mungo had set up their own homes around the hallowed ground that Mungo had set aside for the Lord. The feeling they had just from being near Mungo strengthened their close community so much that a hamlet started to appear around the church – the beginning of Glashgu (later to be the city of Glasgow). Mungo set about allotting tasks and teaching them all about working the land. The monks of those days were skilled in many arts of farming, woodworking and education. Mungo taught the peasants these skills, enabling them to grow more food for the ever-increasing fold, to build better homes and to teach the children.

He selected some that he knew to have been called by God to enter into the priesthood of the Lord. With the land now being looked after by many hands, Mungo spent more time with these disciples, teaching them to read, write and understand the teaching of the Lord Jesus Christ. One day they would need these skills when they themselves were sent out to spread the faith.

During this time Elidyr was still busy fighting the pagan hordes, led by that most evil of men the tyrant Morken the Accursed; they were a constant thorn in his side. It was a few months later before he sent once again his emissaries to check up on Mungo's progress. On arriving, they were surprised at the size of the hamlet that had sprung up. Speaking with Mungo, they pleaded with him to come to see the King, as he was in desperate need of his counselling. Mungo, after feeding and resting the emissaries, sent them back, telling them to inform the King that he would be there by his side within the week to break bread with him.

The morning air was crisp and frost hung from the trees; the land had taken on a new white coat with the approach of winter. Mungo, who was always first to be up, knelt down and thanked the Lord for watching over him in his sleep and for all the graces that he might receive that day. Then he went down to the little burn. Walking into the middle of it, he knelt down and, raising his hands to the heavens, asked the Lord to cleanse his weakness and remove any doubts his body may betray. Some of Mungo's followers were watching and were astonished when he lowered himself under the water. They had seen him do this on other mornings, but that day was different. Ice had formed at the edges of the burn – this was not a morning to submerge oneself as Mungo had done. As they watched, they could feel a sensation flow through them, as though through Mungo's penance in the cold water their own sins were being forgiven. Mungo stood up and walked out of the water – this was not the first time they had seen the miracle of how the Lord had dried Mungo even as he left the water. They all ran down to greet him, and it was now that they could see the glow of saintliness surrounding him. Falling to their knees, one of the ones chosen for the priesthood said, 'The Almighty Lord has sent us a saint who has been truly blessed by His divine Spirit.'

Giving them his blessings, Mungo told them, 'You too can

share in the glory of the Lord if you heed his teachings and never stray from His path. Pray every day to the Holy Mother to intercede with the Lord for you. When I say the Lord is with you, He really is with you and counts you as His own. For those who stray from His path, a fate awaits them that they will wish they had never been born.' Pausing, he then said, 'Arise now; go and prepare and together we will start our journey on the Lord's mission.'

After nourishment, Mungo and his followers set out to travel the distance to meet with the good King of the Britons. All the way there Mungo would sing psalms and his followers would repeat them after him. Following by the great River Clyde, the distance to Dumbarton is approximately eighteen miles. Some of the disciples were not as fit as others, so they progressed at a leisurely pace; brief stops for liquid and food meant that they reached the fortification of Dumbarton in late afternoon. Mungo decided to send on a messenger to alert the King that he was on his way and that he would visit early the next morning. All that night, until sleep overtook them, they listened to the teachings of Jesus, read and explained by Mungo. Many had often wondered how he was able to converse in many local tongues. A mixture of Pict, Angle, Saxon, and Celts had settled in these lands, all with their own tongues. Mungo, like the Lord's blessed Apostles before him, had the gift bequeathed on him by the Almighty Lord, who was pleased with His chosen disciple.

Before the cock crowed, Mungo was, as ever, up saying his prayers. It was said that Mungo hardly slept for more than a few moments at a time, and could be heard saying his prayers and singing psalms throughout the night. It was still very dark, and the morning was cold; it took the disciples a little longer to arouse themselves. By the time they had said their morning prayers and had something to eat, the rays of the morning sun broke through the darkness and the clouds above were dressed in gold as though the angels had painted the sky for the special day. As they started their journey of the last few miles, the sun climbed ever higher in the sky melted the frost; the land was putting on the best of its dresses. As they approached the huge mound that was the fortress of the King, they could see a crowd gathering at the main entrance. Loud horns were blaring out, welcoming their honoured guests. It was at last the day that Elidyr the Handsome had been praying for all these years.

By the time Mungo had reached the main gate, Elidyr, dressed in all his finery, came hurrying out to meet his honoured guest. Approaching Mungo he noticed a spiritual glow surrounding the holy man's head; this was the Lord's way of showing the people that Mungo was a chosen son of the Lord. The King, kneeling before Mungo, asked for his blessing: this was the mark of one who had stayed faithful even against all the trials and tribulations that had gone before. For now the King's only thoughts were for Mungo's mission in his kingdom. Seeing how the King showed his respect for Mungo, the whole gathering knelt down before this saintly man. Mungo offered up a prayer of thanks to the Lord for having brought him here. After blessing all the people, the King escorted Mungo into the fortress's great hall where a feast was laid out. In the good Christian tradition all the people, rich and poor, were invited. The entire population had worked together to make this a special day to remember.

The Glashgu Mission

After the feast, Elidyr led Mungo into an old chapel which had not seen a preacher in many a day. This was the place where the King would often go to seek divine wisdom through prayer. For many a long day he had agonised that the Lord had not heard his pleas and, as he was getting on in years, the wisdom of someone better than he was needed in the matter of his successor. He had two sons, neither of whom had the same faith in Christianity as he, so the counsel of Mungo was most urgent.

Before Mungo listened to the King, he ordered his disciples to make ready the chapel so that they could hold solemn mass to ask the Lord for guidance. Mungo spent all that day hearing about the King's struggles to keep back the pagan foes. Even though Mungo had not travelled very far from the abbey at Culross before coming to this land, he was wise beyond his years; it was a wisdom that had been given to him from above. He counselled the King on what he should do and told him to put his trust in the Lord God Almighty.

Mungo took his leave of the King and went out among the people who had been waiting all day to hear the man of God. They were not disappointed – Mungo stood on the steps high above the people and preached from his Bible. The emotions of some got so strong that they pressed forward just to try to touch him, hoping that in some way their sins might be forgiven.

Realising this, Mungo called out to the Lord, 'Lord, see how Your people long for their deliverance from those who would persecute them. Strengthen their love for You and for one another. Forgive them their sins as they are like little children who have not had Your divine guidance for a long time.'

With his arms outstretched, Mungo blessed them by making the sign of the cross over their heads. As he did so the setting sun turned the skies golden and sent out rays that stretched over their heads, as though sending a message to the people of the east to let them know that God's love fills the whole world. The people lifted up their hands and praised the Lord's name for all His benevolence. Mungo continued to pray with the people for some time. As the night was getting cold, he sent them on their way home, telling them, 'Go home and pray for deliverance that the Lord will fill your hearts and souls with the Holy Spirit, and honour the Holy Mother in prayer. Over the next few days, my brethren, I will stay for a while longer and read some more Scripture about Jesus our Saviour.'

After one week had passed, Mungo had spent most of his time administering the sacraments to the people and counselling the King. The King had confided in Mungo about his two sons; his dilemma was that his oldest son, who was the rightful heir to the throne, wasn't as religious as the younger brother, Rydderck Hael, but was stronger and better soldier. The youngest son, on the other hand, being versed in religious teachings, although not as physically strong, was much wiser. Mungo's advice to the King was to make his youngest son his heir but to make the oldest son his champion of his armies; this pleased the King and the two brothers accepted their father's ruling.

The older brother knew that Mungo was a very wise man and, one day, approached him to tell him that, although he wasn't deeply interested in religion, he respected his father's wishes and vowed to protect the people whatever their faith. Mungo blessed him and told him that even in the old times the Lord had used men in many ways to protect the faith. These men were called the knight protectors of the people and were among the most blessed of men.

As the days passed, Mungo became impatient to return to his new home. On the trip back to Glashgu Mungo's group was swelled by those who decided to follow Mungo. All the way psalms were sung and a carnival atmosphere kept the followers from wearying. By the time they reached the settlement of Glashgu it was late evening. On hearing of the arrival of their beloved pastor with a following of people, the elders ran out to meet them with praises to the Lord for returning their beloved leader safely. As was the tradition in those days the new followers were welcomed, sleeping quarters were made ready and food was shared. Glashgu was growing and spreading its wings.

The winter was quite severe that year and Mungo spent the time instructing his students in the lessons from the Holy Bible. The celebration of the birth of the Lamb of God that year was the first most of the parishioners had had. In his sermons Mungo taught them all about Joseph and Mary, and how they had to travel all the way to Bethlehem in order to fulfil the prophecies as foretold in the Old Testament.

In his own words, Mungo told his students of the prophecy, reinforcing the teachings by saying, 'From you, Oh Bethlehem, a light will be born that will shine over the entire world. A light that will vanquish all the darkness of sins in the world, laying the path you must follow in order to reach your heavenly home. He will be the Lord of all lords, The King of all kings.' The celebrations were of a very simple kind, as the full meaning of the story of Christmas had not been fully absorbed into the worshippers' hearts. In time, and with the guidance of Mungo, the celebration of Christmas at this time of the year would take on a greater meaning and devotions to the Holy Virgin Mary, Mother of Our Lord and the baby Jesus would be celebrated with the reverence they deserved.

Over the next few years in Glashgu, Mungo renewed the faith of whoever would listen. The Druids began to seek out Mungo and ask for his council on matters of religion; they, too, began to convert to Christianity. Once again Mungo absorbed some of the Druidic customs into his own practice and changed them over to a more Christian way. The first years under the reign of Elidyr were when the foundations of a solid Christian Church was laid, so much so that Mungo and his deacons were able to travel far without hindrance. They found in some places that the faith Saint Ninian had established years before was still practised by small pockets of devout Christians, and that there were even a few monks who had been consecrated by Saint Ninian's own monks still preaching the gospel, but few parishioners. When news reached the faithful of a new holy man who was performing miracles and re-establishing the faith, they rejoiced and were encouraged to increase their own efforts in the spreading of the faith that their own Saint Ninian had started many years before.

On one of Mungo's many visits to counsel Elidyr on matters of religion and politics, the King, who had long wished that Mungo would be the father in religion they all craved for, expressed his dearest wish that Mungo accept the position of bishop of Cambria. Mungo resisted, saying that he was too young and not experienced for such a prestigious position. The King was undaunted and sent an emissary to Ireland to plead for a bishop to travel to Glashgu and thereby consecrate Mungo a bishop of the whole area. As was the custom of these days, one bishop would suffice to carry out this sacred deed. In time a bishop who had been ordained by Saint Patrick arrived on these shores with the prime duty to convince Mungo to accept the high position of bishop to the Kingdom of Cambria. This would not be an easy task, as Mungo felt this high office would restrict his calling to convert the pagans. It was only the persuasive power of the King and the clergy that brought the realisation home to Mungo that this was the Lord's way of telling him that this was his destined time to take on a new mantle.

When the great day arrived, people travelled from far and wide just to see who this holy man was that was to become their spiritual leader, whose high office was high above even the highest Druid priest. This was indeed a powerful signal to the rest of the pagans that Christianity had truly arrived in their lives. Darkness had been lifted from their eyes and from this day they would see everything in a new way, even through all the trials to come; their lives would never be the same again. It is said that Mungo was the youngest ever bishop; he was around twenty-seven or twenty-eight years of age. After he was consecrated a bishop, he set about driving the final effigies and shrines to the demons of paganism out. He then started setting up parishes and had churches built. Deacons and priests were ordained; unlawful marriages were dissolved. The practice of having more than one wife was from that time stopped. The pagans of the Clyde Valley took to Christianity because it offered them hope of a better life, free from persecution and slavery from the strongest warlords.

Far to the south-east, news reached the ears of one of the vilest of pagan kings about the rise of Christianity and of this new preacher called Mungo. Morken the Accursed was his name. He, it was said, was against Christianity in any form and sworn to rid the kingdom of it once he had conquered this land. While he was preparing his armies to invade the northern lands, a stroke of good fortune came his way. News arrived of the death of Elidyr, which had thrown the kingdom into turmoil; this was his signal to unleash his murdering marauders on the kingdom.

He met no resistance until he was deep into what is now the Strathclyde area. Here he came face to face with the young King Rydderck Hael and his older brother who led the army. The battle was violent and bloody, with Morken gaining the upper hand and with Rydderck Hael's brother slain. Rydderck Hael's army was then in disarray; they fled in all directions. Rydderck Hael himself escaped north to lick his wounds. The result of this battle was that Morken became the undisputed ruler of the Cambrian kingdom and so began darkness over the land.

At this time Mungo was away on pastoral duties and had not heard the news about the change of rulers or even of the death of Elidyr. When news of the battle finally reached him and he learned who the new king was, he hurried back to his beloved Glashgu with all haste. These were uncertain days for the fledgling faith, so much so that some of the weaker in faith fled back to their old abodes before Mungo returned, fearing reprisal from Morken. Mungo's first duty was to strengthen their faith. He told them always to trust in the Lord. The wicked, he said, would one day be punished by the Almighty God. This was the first time his followers had seen such a saintly aura of confidence surrounding their master.

After the battle, Morken and his men plundered and raped the land, stealing anything of value, slaying anyone who stood in their way. After they had had their fill, they returned to their stronghold in the south, only leaving small garrisons to keep the people under heel. For a short while all was calm and people started to relax, but before long marauding soldiers of Morken's army came back demanding tax by way of food, oxen, grain and valuables. One day a band of braggarts arrived at the hamlet of Glashgu, demanding more than the people could afford to give. Mungo faced them down and, through his will, forced them to retreat.

This was only short-lived, however, as a few weeks later a much stronger army arrived. They forcibly took every piece of food, including all the harvested grain and corn that had been gathered from the fields, leaving nothing, not even a single seed to sow crops for the coming year. This could not have come at a worse time, as the seeds had to be sown within the next few days. The elders approached Mungo, asking what they could do.

Mungo told them, 'Put your faith in the Lord and He will provide. Remember this day, I tell you, the Lord will in his own time smite your enemies and bring down those who offend Him.'

But the cries of the people started to bear down so hard on Mungo that he took himself off into the woods where he could be alone with his Lord.

He knelt in prayer. 'Lord,' he said, 'hear my plea and give me a sign that my flock will see that You in all Your magnificence have not abandoned them.' As he knelt praying, a few grains of corn appeared before him. 'Lord I am not sure what You would have me to do with so few seeds when I have such a large flock to feed,' he said.

The voice of an angel spoke to him, telling him he was to mix the seeds with sand and sow them over the whole field. Mungo obeyed the wishes of the Lord. Returning to the hamlet, he called the elders together. What he asked them to do was beyond their belief, but having seen so many wonders performed by Mungo they carried out his will with obedience. Mixing the few seed grains with sand, they presented their work before Mungo who prayed over them and blessed the seeds and the sand. Then he took them and sowed them in the field.

Weeks later, all over the field the young corn burst through the earth and reached up, as though in praise of the Almighty Lord. On seeing this, the elders could not believe their own eyes; not one inch of the field was barren. With hands held high and falling to their knees, they gave praise and thanks to the Lord for sending Mungo to be their leader, who was surely a great saint and whom the Lord had blessed. That year's was the best crop they ever harvested; they had more than enough for everyone in the hamlet and some to spare to feed the people of the surrounding area.

Their happiness did not last for long once Mungo had gone to carry out his duties for the Lord. The news of abundant grain soon reached Morken's men and they came back, stealing all that the people had worked for. The soldiers took all they could carry; and travelling along the River Clyde they stored the grain in big sheds near the riverside. When he returned and found that this had happened, Mungo was furious that they should steal all that the Lord had provided for his people. He called upon the Lord to invoke the river to swell and overflow; to lift up the grain his people had worked so hard for and carry it all back up stream to Glashgu. That night while the soldiers slept, the great River Clyde swelled over the banks right up to the grain sheds. Lifting the grain, the flow of the river carried it upstream and left the grain high and dry on the banks of the Molendinar Burn. The next morning, when the people saw with their own eyes that the Lord had indeed listened to his chosen son and had by a miracle returned all the grain that had been stolen, they held a service in thanksgiving. That was the last time the small hamlet of Glashgu would ever again be persecuted by Morken's men.

Learning of these mysterious events, Morken denounced Mungo as a sorcerer and a magician. He was unable to understand that Mungo was only carrying out the Lord's will. In vengeance, for the next few years Morken stepped up the persecution of the outer lands, but he dared not go near the lands under Mungo's administration. Morken believed in his twisted mind that Mungo was trying to take his place as ruler and king of all the Cambria; he could not understand that Mungo only wanted to save souls for the Almighty Lord.

The cries from the persecuted people of the outer lands started to reach Mungo. As he often did when he needed to think and be closer to God, Mungo went off into solitude to search his heart for an answer. After thirty days of solitude he returned to his people. He called them together and told them the Lord wanted him to go and speak to Morken, just as Moses had done when he went to confront the Pharaoh in Egypt, and Daniel when he entered the lions' den. Mungo, however, would have to face the demons in their own home. At first the elders tried to persuade him not to go, for fear he would not return, but they found out that when the call from the Lord told Mungo to go somewhere, his obedience was total.

During the next few days of preparation for the journey, the elders were assembled by Mungo and instructed to prepare the land near the first church they had erected for the building of a larger church, because the old church had become too small for all the new parishioners. To be built at the same time was a building with quarters for the many monks who had now been ordained. After saying solemn mass, it was agreed that some of the holiest of the monks, twelve in number, would accompany Mungo on his historic journey to meet Morken. As with the Apostles, they took only the clothes they wore and their faith, with the belief that the Lord would provide for them.

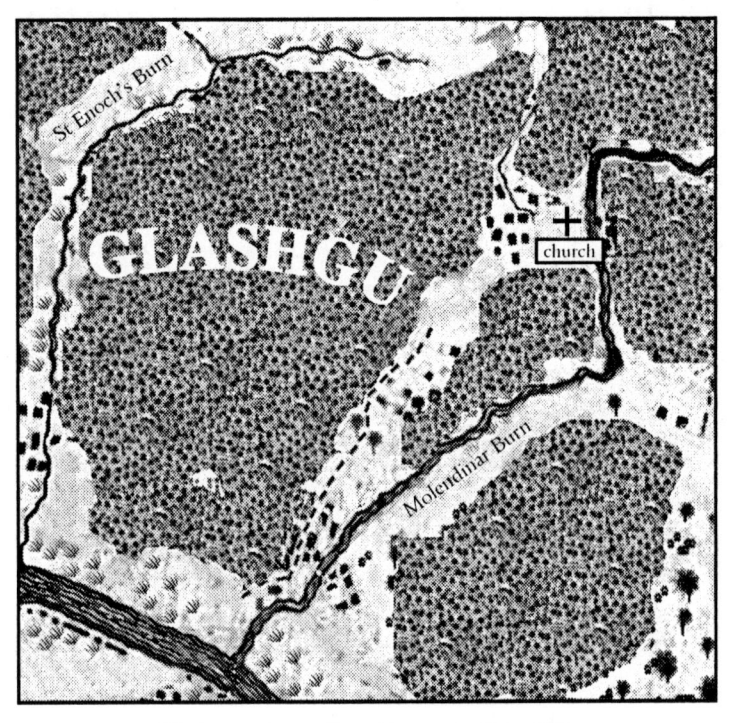

Glashgu as it may have been around AD 550.

1752 map of Glasgow digitally altered by kind permission of the National Map Library and Museum of Scotland

Mungo faces his Foe

Through out all Mungo's travels no harm had ever befallen him, for the Lord had always protected his chosen son. But this trip was somewhat different, as the Lord hadn't taken Mungo into his confidence, so it was with some trepidation that the holy band headed south into the land ravaged by the pagan hordes. Singing as they went and chanting holy psalms, at the start most were full of the joys of life, heading off on a great adventure for the first time. That was until they began to pass dwellings that had been ransacked. Their mood changed a little; this was when their faith would be tested to the full. Wherever they stopped, people would come out from the woods seeking a blessing from the saint they had heard about. This was new territory for Mungo; his mission was to convert to Christianity all who would hear the word of the Lord.

His journey south into the area now known as Castle O'er Forest, near Eskdalemuir, took longer than he expected, as many small hamlets had not heard the word of the Lord Jesus for a long time. To the people it was a breath of fresh air to hear the Scriptures again preached by a saintly man such as Mungo. News spread and the people found the courage to come out of hiding. Some of the younger monks were overwhelmed by the people's gratitude – food was brought forward to nourish the travellers and fresh milk to quench their thirst. This was as Mungo always told them: 'Have faith and the Lord will provide.'

For Mungo, spreading the word of the Lord Jesus and being among the people was what he had been born to do. To the unconverted poor souls who were in need of hope, he gave much more – he was a spark sent by the Lord to rekindle their dormant faith and give them the will to start over again. Doing the Lord's work also strengthened Mungo's resolve to overcome the pangs of doubt at facing the evil Morken.

All along his journey, the people greeted Mungo. It was like a new dawn for them. The radiance he exuded lit up the way, a beacon for the people made pure by the hands of the Almighty. Word had spread about Mungo's journey even before his entourage reached the hamlets on his way. Mungo could see the people's longing for a saviour in their eyes; they wanted someone to speak out for them. Along the way he instructed the monks who travelled with him and appointed some to stay at various places to administer the sacraments to the people.

The journey south was long. In those days, Mungo travelled on foot, never accepting the convenience of a cart pulled by bullocks, and the monks who were still with him learned how to endure the physical pain of such a long journey on the road. Their admiration for their leader grew stronger as each day passed. Mungo did not flinch or ever seem tired; he gave encouragement by singing psalms and quoting from the Scriptures as they walked. After a time only four monks were still travelling with him.

Into the deep south of the kingdom, it was evident that they were nearing Morken's stronghold. The Lord though had hidden Mungo's journey from the eyes of this barbarous King, so much so that Mungo's entourage was nearly at O'er Fortress before the King was told. Morken was amused at such a stupid attempt from this magician to appear before him. Calling his guards, he mockingly sent out a band of his cut-throats to escort Mungo and his group into the very heart of his evil lair.

When they met, Mungo found Morken sitting on a huge throne; the décor of the room was befitting the savages they were. The King was courteous in a sarcastic way, but his bravado did not fool Mungo. Mocking Mungo, the King asked him to do some tricks for those assembled, saying 'I hear you are a great sorcerer and have done many tricks to pull the wool over the weak in mind. Do some for me so that I may reward you.'

Standing in the centre of the room with his staff in one hand and his holy book in the other, Mungo said, 'Do not mock this humble servant of the Lord Jesus Christ. I come here to plead for my people, not to test the Lord, for it is written that anyone who tests the Lord our God will suffer damnation in the fires of hell.'

Morken laughed. 'Fool, do you think I, the mighty Morken,

fear this figment of your imagination? I have crushed mightier men than you.'

Mungo replied, 'I have not come to confront your leadership, only to ask with humility that you let the people live in peace, to ask you to share the food with the poor and the starving. The Lord will in all his glory bless you if you do this thing; if not, the Lord's revenge will be more than all the pain you can imagine, more than the grief you have given your subjects.'

Morken was furious and stamped down from his throne. Standing in front of Mungo and looking into his eyes, he said, 'I am the only almighty king in these parts, and no one tells me what I should do, not even your God!'

Mungo had looked into men's eyes before, but had never seen such evil as he saw now. Summoning up all his courage, he repeated his plea for the people. Morken was even more furious that such a demand should be made to him; he lashed out with his right boot, kicking Mungo to the ground. Turning his back on Mungo with a wave of disdain, he said, 'Away with you, and take your weak-minded band with you. You are not worthy of the effort to kill you.' Everyone except the monks laughed and poured more scorn on Mungo and his followers.

Two of the monks ran forward and helped their leader to his feet. Feeling that he had failed, Mungo turned and led his entourage out. As they started back the way they had come, there was a silence that hadn't been there before. Deep in thought, Mungo could have been on his own walking that road. On they walked until Mungo stopped. Gathering his disciples around him, he told them to carry on back to Glashgu. He told them he had to meditate on his own and ask for guidance from the Lord, and would be some time away.

He felt confused after his meeting with Morken, and felt humiliated by the treatment he had received. This was a new experience for him, as the Lord had always protected him wherever he went. Mungo travelled into the wilderness until an angel called on him to stop. As he knelt, it was clear to the Lord that his favoured son was hurting after his confrontation with the evil king. All that day, the Lord spoke words to Mungo through an angel, calming his fears and impressing on him that He had heard his pleas; the evildoing of Morken would be punished before the next day was out.

The Lord's justice was swift. The very next day the evil tyrant was out hunting for wild boar, feeling superior in himself and overconfident of his horsemanship, showing off to his fellow hunters. In his boastful fashion he tried to force his horse to jump over a huge tree that had fallen down. The Lord commanded the horse to stumble and throw its rider. Hearing the Lord, the horse obeyed and the evil king was thrown; he travelled through the air and was impaled on a sharp branch that the Lord had prepared for him. Feeling the pain, Morken saw his life pass before his eyes. With his last breath he saw the Lord in all his glory, only for his soul to be ripped away and dispatched to his master, the Devil, whom he had worshipped so much. The Lord had teased the dying king with a vision of what he could have had; and rewarded him with what he deserved.

Mungo received a vision of the King's death, and of the justice the Lord would hand out to anyone who should try to defile His chosen ones. Mungo stayed in the wilderness for a while before continuing his journey home. Meanwhile, the news of Morken's death spread throughout the kingdom and there was rejoicing all over the land. The monks had no doubt that the hand of God had interceded on their behalf.

Back in Morken's stronghold, disbelief prevailed. Arguments broke out even before the King's body was burned (as was the sacrificial custom of the pagans) and fighting was rife between the different factions. The inheritance of the crown was not always through heredity means and most of the time it was the most brutal who succeeded – this was the way it had always been. With the leadership in turmoil, bands of cut-throats and thieves plundered at will throughout the land, trying to carve out little kingdoms of their own.

After what seemed ages, Mungo returned to a tumultuous welcome in Glashgu. Mungo's dear people all believed that God's will, through Mungo, had changed the course of history. In the months since Mungo had left, the township of Glashgu had become even bigger; the building of the new church and living quarters were well underway. The head elder came to Mungo and thanked him for giving them the tasks he had commanded them to do; this, he said, had pulled them together as one community. It had also taken away their doubts that the Lord would, in His wisdom, look over their beloved leader. Mungo was very pleased with all the progress that was being made and thanked the Lord for his patience.

After a while, word come to Mungo and his flock that a new king had been settled on, by the name of Cynfarch Oer, (Oer means 'the Dismal'). This king was not one for the Christians to celebrate over, as he was a descendent of Morken the Accursed. Although not as brutal as the previous king, he nevertheless still had a great dislike for Mungo. Cynfarch believed that Mungo was responsible for the death of Morken through sorcery and he swore on his coronation day to avenge his former king. Cynfarch, though, was afraid of an outright confrontation with Mungo. With his fellow conspirators he deviously drew up a plan to persecute the believers of Christianity in the outlying lands, hoping that this would turn the people against Mungo and they might then drive him out.

The dwellings that now made up the township of Glashgu were having a peaceful time and beginning to prosper. Fear of Mungo had kept the barbaric hordes away from their door. In the outlying lands, though, things were much more different: in some cases, monks were put to death solely because of their faith. Many men were martyred at this time and were later made saints. Fear of reprisals was always in the minds of the people. During this period the marauders forced many areas back into pagan rituals, and rape and death became common events.

Hearing the cries of his people, Mungo sought a sign from the Lord. 'What must I do?' he asked when he prayed. The Lord's answer was not forthcoming and the cries grew louder. Calling the town elders and his disciples together, he explained that he had to go away to seek out the Lord for answers to his dilemma. He promised he would not desert them in their time of need. After giving out commands and instructions as to what had to be done in his absence, he held mass for the persecuted people, asking the Lord to ease their burden and to help them keep their faith alive. For his own dear people, he asked the Lord to strengthen their will and to give them the strength to repel any marauding band who should try to persecute them. He left his most learned monks in charge of the community and the Holy Sacraments. With this done, he blessed all who were assembled there and took his leave of them.

The Morken's castle, where Saint Mungo faced his evil enemies, has not been placed on any historical map. Castle O'er, though, is situated in Castle O'er Forest, near Eskdalemuir on the B709 road to Langholm. Battles have been fought around this area throughout history. In all probability this was a fortress of the pagan kings around this period.

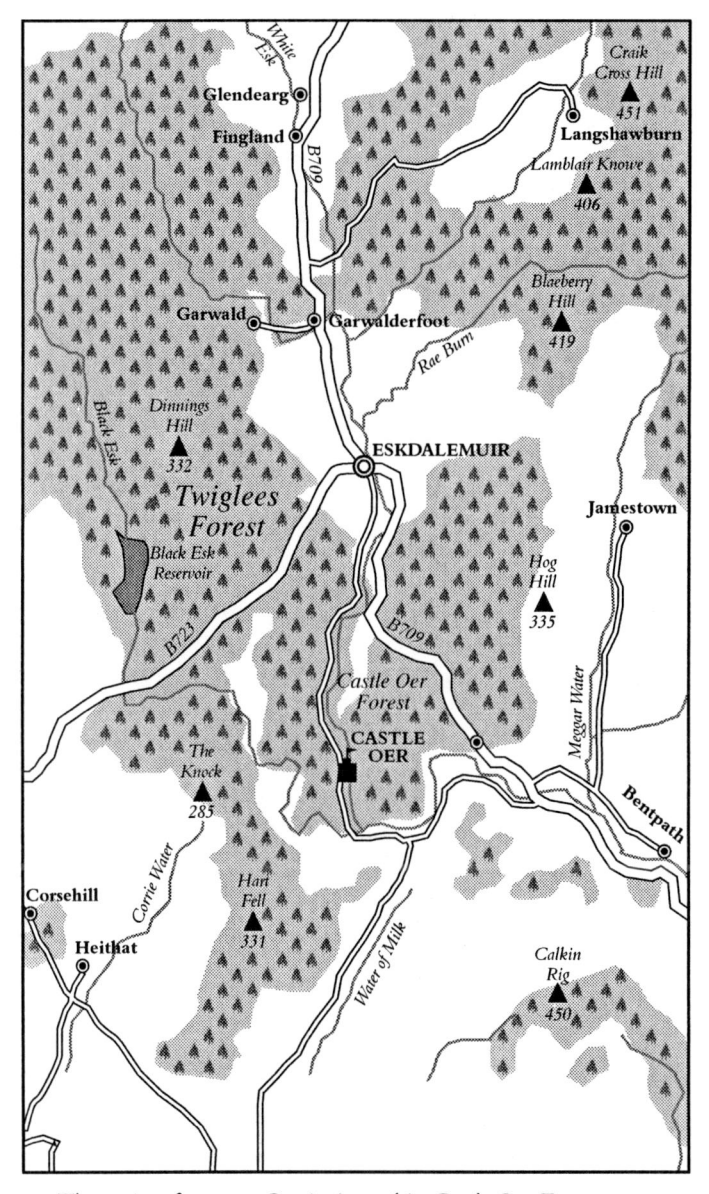

The ancient fortress at Oer is situated in Castle Oer Forest, near Eskdalemuir on the B709

Conquering of Doubts

The direction Mungo took was north, up into the mountains, where he could be alone with his thoughts, and seek out the answers to the question that lay before him. Higher and higher he climbed until he was above the tree line. It was cold and wet and there was no protection against the elements; this, he thought, would get him closer to the Lord.

For days he wandered without any sign from the Lord. In his anguish Mungo felt very alone and, like all men, he felt that he was nothing without the Lord's comfort. At his weakest, he asked, 'Lord why have You forsaken me when I am in need of Your council?'

One day he came upon a cave and decided to stop there, praying constantly, with hardly any respite. After this, for the next forty days, Mungo wandered over the mountains, avoiding contact with all other humans, his only company the herds of wild deer that inhabited the region. One stag stood proud like a heavenly guard among the herd and seemed to keep watch over him, but in his confused state he did not notice.

These were trying times for Mungo. His despair grew deeper because he could not hear the Lord's soothing words of comfort. Feeling lost and abandoned, he wondered if the Lord had tired of him, or if he had offended God, who had always kept him on the path that He had destined for him. Living on wild plants and drinking only from small pools of rainwater, he started to see apparitions of what might be and what could be for his great land: battles and pestilence, turmoil, paganism and shifting borders, but all through this, at times, he saw peace and prosperity, and Christianity flourishing and gaining a foothold in the hearts of men. In this way, the Lord cleansed Mungo of his doubts. After a while of solitude, the Lord in His wisdom sent an angel to console him and to build back up his strength for the tasks ahead. The angel allowed Mungo to see into the future; he saw all the things the Lord had ordained and the missions that Mungo would carry out; but even then he still felt he was unworthy of the Lord's benevolence to him. As time went by his faith strengthened in the Lord and he could feel His presence all around him. Even in the stormiest weather he basked in the glory of the Lord and walked only in sunshine.

By the end of Mungo's self-exile, the Lord had purged all doubts from his heart and had purified his soul. He was now cleansed, ready to get back to his beloved mission of Glashgu. It was not going to be an easy task to tell his dear people of the Lord's intentions for him, of the sacrifices he and his people would have to make.

Once out of the mountains, Mungo was met by some of his beloved monks. He did not know that because of their love for their blessed leader, these monks had followed him all the way to the foot of the mountains. Here they had built a little altar and prayed to the Lord to bless their holy bishop that he might impart on them the blessing of love and understanding that He, in all His magnificence, would shower on those who feared Him.

On the road home to Glashgu, Mungo would stop and, as he was charged by the Lord to do, would convert and baptise all who would hear the calling of the Lord. When he reached his beloved Glashgu, throngs of people assembled to greet him, and his homecoming was welcomed by the monks and the elders. When they looked at him they could see a new radiance surrounding him like a divine halo. The procession led Mungo all the way to the front of the newly-completed larger church; he was very pleased that the fruits of his labour had finally been harvested. By this time the population of Glashgu was rapidly swelling, so much so that it was now one of the largest townships in the land.

With great joy in his heart Mungo turned to speak to the people, but so many had turned up that those at the back could not see or hear. To the multitude's astonishment, Mungo appeared to rise up into the skies. Folklore has it that Mungo ordered the ground to rise up into a mound so that all the people could see him and know that it was with the blessing of the Son of God, the Lord Jesus Christ, that he was granted the power to perform these miracles. Once the entire congregation had quietened down,

Mungo raised his hands up to the Lord in heaven and spoke.

'Lord, see the people's need for Your love; let Your holy light shine down and bless all who are here. Let Your strength be their strength and always guide their hearts to the path that leads them to You, Father in heaven. Always protect them in their hour of need, watch over them while I do Your will and, dear Lord, by the praising of Your name let Glashgu flourish for Your glory for ever. Amen.'

Mungo spent the next few hours preaching the holy gospel to the crowds and walking among them, laying his hand on the heads of all the little children and blessing them, as he knew that these were the future of the Christian Church, the Church that from this day on would grow. Sending them all home, he asked them to return the next day when the new church would be consecrated to Almighty Lord.

After the next day's ceremony, Mungo started to prepare his monks for his imminent departure. Although most did not know what was going on, some had been taken into Mungo's confidence and the preparations to organise the structure of the town's clergy started to take shape. Mungo bestowed higher office on his most trusted monks and promoted some to the missions. Calling together all the elders, as there were a large number now that Glashgu had grown so much, he divided the town into smaller sections and bestowed mayorship on his most faithful and trusted follower. He elected and instructed a council to deal with all things to do with the general life of the people. The laws would be handed down from the Church as taught by the Lord Jesus Christ. Thus Mungo set in motion the morals and the commerce for the development of the now growing Glashgu.

The days passed while Mungo carried out his task of organisation and he was pleased with what he saw. The missionary work to spread the Christian faith further was being received by the people, but Cynfarch Oer, the king was making life very difficult for his young priests. Some were badly beaten up, others were humiliated and all were sent back to Mungo with the same message: the persecution would continue until Mungo left the kingdom.

But Mungo had not yet finished the preparations for the systems he wanted to introduce. He grieved for the pain his followers had to suffer, but knew that the Lord's work must be done as He willed.

A few weeks after that most glorious day in front of the new church, while Mungo was singing his psalms an angel appeared and told him of the Lord's commands. The angel told him that because he was in danger he was to make preparations to leave with all haste. So the next day Mungo told his most trusted monks of the Lord's command and charged them to carry on the work they had begun, to stay faithful to the teachings of the Lord Jesus, to obey all the Commandments and honour all the holy days in the year.

That day Mungo presided over the Holy Sacraments in what he thought would be his last mass in the new church, the church he was the bishop of. That day, to the great consternation of the people there present, he broke to them the news of the command from the Lord above: that he must leave for the betterment of all. He promised they would always be in his heart and his prayers. He told them that he would return one day, if the Lord allowed.

After all was prepared, Mungo selected a few of his loyal younger monks. The journey was not for the faint-hearted; they would venture into territory untouched by the faith of our Lord, into pagan country. With the guidance of the Lord, they would preach the good word from the Holy Bible and Christianise wherever they found heathens and those who worshipped idols. The angel had told Mungo the direction that he should take in order to bypass those who would persecute him. The journey south began around the year AD 555. Mungo and his small band said their farewells to the people. Everyone was sorrowful at seeing their beloved bishop take his leave of them; for many this would be the last time they would see Saint Mungo, as they now thought of him, until they met again in the house of the Almighty God, our heavenly Father.

It is said that Glasgow grew and prospered even when Saint Mungo was away fulfilling his missions in the name of the Lord Jesus Christ. Glasgow grew more rapidly than any other area of Scotland and from early days was a hub of commerce. This can be put down to the gift of knowledge that Saint Mungo imparted on to his fellow men, and also to the people's faith and hard work. Maybe that's the reason the pagan hoards did not ransack the fledgling town – why bite the hand that feeds you? Through fear or superstition of Saint Mungo, it would appear the pagans preferred trade to confrontation.

Christianity took hold very quickly in the Glasgow area; this was most surely down to Saint Mungo and the people's desire for a better life than the one they had. Friendship and sharing were all part of the early Christian faith; this idea brought like-minded men to settle under the protection of Glasgow's patron saint, Saint Mungo.

Mungo's Mission South

As if cloaked by an invisible shield, Mungo and his entourage travelled undetected by the pagan bands that were roaming the land looking for them. The Lord only allowed them to be seen when they were near people of Christian beliefs. As was his way, Mungo would often spend time with these people, administering the sacraments, but move on before the King's men got word of his presence. On his way south, Mungo performed many miracles, healing of the sick and giving hope to the old and infirm, preaching as he went and spreading the gospel of the Lord Jesus to anyone whose soul was open to the word of God.

It was in the spring of AD 556 when they reached the town of Karleolum (Carlisle), once a main Roman town on the western end of Hadrian's Wall. Karleolum had a Christian population of size, and its own bishop. Word had reached the people of Karleolum that a chosen son of God, a man called Mungo who was praised as Kentigern, meaning 'head priest', was on his way to their city. Passing through the gates of Hadrian's Wall, Mungo and his followers were met with great enthusiasm and welcomed into the town. In those days Karleolum had a great cathedral-size church, situated right in the town centre. The Bishop, dressed in very fine clothes, was at the front of the welcoming committee whose hospitality overwhelmed the pious Mungo and his group. But Mungo's first impression of the Bishop of Karleolum was not very good. He felt that he was too ostentatious and that the faith of the people may have been diluted by this show of importance, and may have relaxed the true Christian values of the clergy and people. Mungo believed in total obedience to the Lord in everything; that one should be a servant of the people and never indulge at all in the pleasure of vanity. His only thoughts were of following the teachings of the Lord Jesus Christ.

The Bishop, listening to Mungo's first sermons the very next day, felt as though he was hearing the Scriptures for the first time.

His soul was lifted up with a new awareness of what he must do. From that moment he knew that this was no ordinary preacher – Mungo's sermons hit hard, deep into his soul. The congregation felt the same way. Mungo's words renewed and strengthened the faith in the souls that were weak and to brought into the fold those who were lost.

Full of admiration, his faith renewed as it should be by all Mungo stood for, the Bishop set about trying to get Mungo to stay a while longer. But Mungo told him that his mission was to seek out and convert to Christianity those poor heathen souls who were ignorant of the true word of the Lord.

Seeing that there was no way he could convince Mungo to stay, the Bishop told Mungo of the many heathen people up in the hills around Karleolum who had refused the Divine Law and Christianisation. They, he told him, still worshipped idols, and followed all the heathen traditions of their ancestors. For years he and many of his clergy had on numerous occasions attempted to convert them, but had been driven away. The Bishop pleaded with Mungo, that he, before continuing his own mission, intercede on his behalf to persuade the heathens to repent and follow the teachings of the Lord Jesus Christ.

Calling together all the priests and clergy of the area, Mungo repeated and laid down the laws that the Lord Jesus had preached. He took them to task over their weakness for the sins of the flesh; he told them to abstain and live only to serve the Lord and the faithful people's souls. Many confessed and were forgiven, but some would not; the Lord would, in His own way, punish them for their disobedience.

After having spent many days in the company of the good folk of Karleolum, Mungo was eager to be about the mission that the Lord had entrusted to him. Before he left, the Bishop charged him to take some of his monks with him, that they might learn from his teachings, and in doing so would be stronger in faith. At the Bishop's request, Mungo left one of his trusted monks behind to help the Bishop re-evangelise his clergy and congregation. A Church of people, Mungo told them, who start to change the Lord's commandments to suit their own needs, like wild animals will bite off their own legs to feed their hunger.

By the time they took their leave of the good folk of Karleolum, Mungo's group had swollen to nearly thirty souls. On the guidance of one of his new fellow travellers, Mungo headed up into the wooded hills of the area known today as the Lake District, into the lands of the misguided unclean souls who waited to hear the word that would set them free. Their journey deep into the forest that spread over the mountains took them through places on the map known today as Caldbeck and Mungrisdale. On they walked until they came to a clearing in the forest under the shadow of Skiddaw mountain; Mungo surveyed the place and decided this would be a good spot to stay. To mark this spot he planted a cross in the middle of the clearing. All who passed would know that the Lord claimed this as a hallowed place. Later this place would be known as Crosthwaite, meaning 'cross in the forest clearing'.

It was not long before word spread about this new challenge to pagan beliefs. First the Druids of the area approached Mungo; in the past they had been able to chase off those who came trying to take their place with other religions. But this time they found that this was no ordinary missionary trying to covert them; this was truly a man of God who was more than a match for their own brand of magic. While they held the people in sway with mysterious tricks, with only a look or a prayer Mungo was able to disarm any that opposed the word of the Lord. Only a few, including some Druids, accepted the Word in the beginning, while others resisted Mungo's preaching. As time passed, like the torrent of water that flows down from the mountaintop on a rainy day, the flow of people to hear and be converted by Mungo grew stronger with each passing day.

After a period of time had passed, Mungo started to send out his disciples among the people, thus spreading the good news far and wide. People started to make pilgrimage to see, and be baptised into the Christian Church at the hands of the one who was called a saint. Mungo had done in a very short time what others could not. With the conversion to the faith of all the local tribes Mungo set about organising the areas into parishes, to be served in some cases by lay preachers, and to be backed up with monks travelling around visiting each parish to administer the

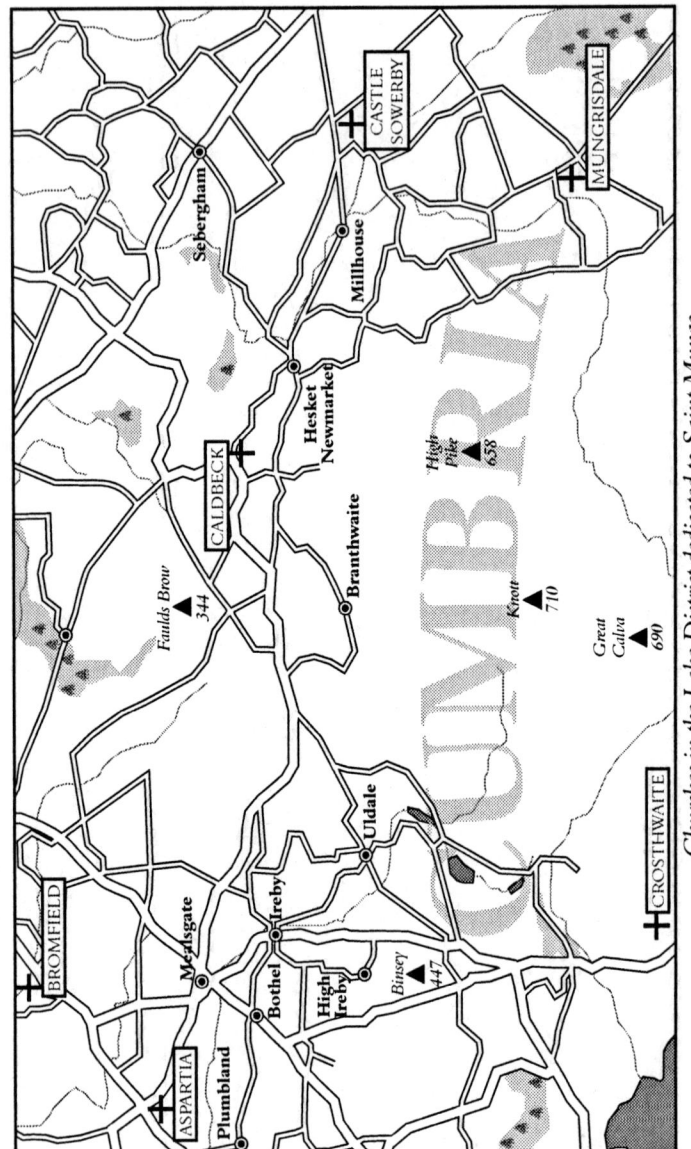

Churches in the Lake District dedicated to Saint Mungo

sacraments. Mungo himself travelled the district consecrating places of worship. In a place known today as Castle Sowerby, Mungo is said to have miraculously sprung a holy well and used its blessed water to baptise many converts to the faith. A church dedicated to Saint Mungo now stands there, while the well, now dry, stands inside the churchyard wall beside the path leading to the house.

Mungo travelled extensively over the district, stopping in places known today as Bromfield and Aspatria. Today churches stand in his honour in these places. How long Saint Mungo spent in this area of the Lake District is unknown, but to have accomplished all that and to be remembered by all the dedications he must have taken the best part of two years. Did he complete his entire mission on foot? It might be said, 'Saint Mungo trod in your light, oh Lord on high, and did many great deeds by miracle.'

This episode of his mission now over, Mungo returned to meet with the Bishop of Karleolum to hand over the land of all the souls that were now singing the praise of the Lord to his safe keeping. The converted area of the Cambrian Lake District had seen a new light. Paganism was all but eradicated from the land, although, as today, some people hid their heads in the fog of hate, which had been their way for generations. These people became outcasts from their nation.

Having accomplished everything that he had set out to do, Mungo said his last mass in the church of Karleolum and left the congregation with some last words of wisdom. He told them, 'The Lord Jesus Christ never said it would be easy to be a good Christian. There are still people who would persecute you all in the name of ignorance, but one must strive to do your best. The Kingdom of Heaven is that which will be the reward for those who do, and they will be all the better off for having tried with all their heart and soul. The Lord in all his mercy loves those who fight to live by his Commandments and strive to overcome their weaknesses.'

A few centuries before Saint Mungo the Roman legions had built the defensive wall and established Carlisle. A huge garrison of soldiers meant that there would have been a fair-sized town by the year AD 556. Christianity was being practised here around this time.

In Cumbria today there are some eight churches dedicated to Saint Mungo, most under the name of Kentigern: to the north of Carlisle in places called Irthington, Kirkcambeck and Grimsdale; in the Lake District, Caldbeck, Mungrisdale (thought to mean 'Valley of Mungo's pigs', as this was a common farm animal then, and the only church dedicated in the name of Mungo); Crosthwaite on the outskirts of Keswick; Castle Sowerby standing alone up on the moors; Bromfield and Aspatria near the coast.

Of Saint Mungo's next journey, which took him to South Wales, no records have been found concerning how he travelled there. Some believe he may have sailed from a point on the coast near Aspatria in Cumbria. This conclusion is supported by the fact there are no areas on the route south where places were dedicated to Mungo or Kentigern, as was the fashion to do so. Others point out that it is always said that he travelled everywhere on foot. Whichever way he went, to the south of Wales he travelled, along with his most trusted disciples.

Meeting Saint David (Dewi)

One day in the Kingdom of Menevia in South Wales, Bishop David (Saint David), while in the monastery church, knelt in front of the altar and, as he prayed, a vision appeared to him in the form of an angel. This angel had come with good news for this saintly man. The news was that soon a chosen son of the Lord would visit him on a mission ordained by God, to fulfil a quest to change the hearts of men for ever in lands far and near.

The Lord's message to David was, 'Give to this servant, with whom I am most pleased, all the help and wisdom you possess. Make him welcome, and nourish and rest him after his long journey. For I, the Lord your God, will one day send this most obedient servant on his way out among the heathens of the land to carry out My will.'

Out of the mists of time, around the year AD 558, strode Mungo with his band of followers, weary after their long journey, into a land they knew not. The Lord had been their guide and saviour all the way. No harm or bad weather had befallen them on their way, as folklore would have it. 'The Lord in his mercy would only let the sunshine fall on His chosen son Mungo and those who stood in his shadow.'

The road they followed took them to what seemed to be a huge man-made hill. Later on, as they passed over the ridge of a small brae, they realised that what they thought was a hill was in fact the monastery built by David. It was the largest monastery they had ever seen.

His heart filled with joy, Mungo praised the Lord for having guided him to this place which surely was blessed. Never had Mungo seen such a magnificent uplifting of prayer to the Almighty God. As they got nearer the village, people who had been foretold of the coming of a servant of the Lord came out waving flowers and singing welcoming psalms. As they came nearer, the monastery seemed to grow larger, until they reached the steps leading up to the main door. Mungo knelt down at journey's end and offered up prayers to the Lord for all He had done for them. The huge doors of the monastery opened and out strode David glowing in the sunlight of the Lord. He walked down the steps and greeted Mungo as if he was his long-lost brother. Embracing, they both stood with their arms around one another, lost in mutual respect. The people and Mungo's disciples all knelt down at once, witness to the outpouring of love sent down from heaven upon two chosen sons of God.

After the welcomes were over, David took Mungo on a tour of the monastery. The sights he beheld that day stayed with him for the rest of his life. The first months of their stay in this wonderful building opened the eyes of Mungo's disciples to the greater glory of the Lord. Mungo spent most of his time in the company of David. They talked endlessly about all that they had done through the Lord's grace and of all the things they would like to accomplish in the Lord's name. These were not ambitions of self-importance, but missions that had been revealed to them by the Lord. David's praise for Mungo grew with each passing day. He began to realise that this man, known lovingly by the people in those parts as Kentigern, was a specially chosen son of the Lord and his light of faith burned brightest of all. David himself was aware of his own favour growing with the blessing they both shared in the Lord.

Over time Mungo had began to realise that he had failed the Lord by not having recorded all that had gone before. When wandering around David's monastery, he saw monks from all over the lands, even from Ireland and Gaul (France), studying and writing things down for the furthering of the faith. He felt that he had failed by neglecting to leave written histories for future generations. Mungo had never been a scholastic type of monk; in his simple way he had spread the gospel of the Lord by his examples: of prayer and humble living; never chastising, always forgiving; serving others before himself and acting towards others with love and kindness and, in return, asking not for himself, but that they should love and obey the Lord.

The Lord in his wisdom had brought Mungo to this place to complete his education in the ways that the Lord wanted him to carry forth the scriptures and to add another sword of truth written down for all who would follow in his footsteps. The time passed and Mungo's feet began to itch for travel again. David, through his talks with Mungo, had learned that he wanted to establish a monastery for the Lord to carry on with the mission the Lord had charged him with. Knowing that Mungo would need land first, David arranged for Mungo to meet the king of that land, a Christian king of great conscience and magnanimity called Cathwallian. The King was overjoyed and so impressed after his meetings with Mungo that he opened his entire kingdom to the saint, telling him, 'Go find the place the Lord desires for you, that the raising of Church and cross for the glory of His name shall spread throughout all the land.'

Legend has it that before Mungo started his quest to find hallowed ground, he made one last trip to meet the legendary king of the Round Table, King Arthur. It is said that Mungo sat at this Round Table with Arthur and his loyal knights and gave counsel. It is also said that Arthur was most impressed by this servant of the church and commissioned Mungo to give counsel whenever he, the King, was in need of matters of the faith. Only legend records this meeting, as well as how, after a long struggle with the magician Merlin, by Mungo's own hands Merlin gave his soul to the Lord in baptism. The mists of time make it hard to say what is truth or legend, but the thread of the life that is the legend of King Arthur will weave through many future events.

Once again Mungo and his followers were saying their farewells, this time with a purpose in mind. They left David, but took away all that they had learned during their long stay and all the good will that the people could give. As a parting gift, David bequeathed to Mungo some of his scribes as future teachers to what would surely be an ever-growing flock.

Travelling in a northerly direction, Mungo used all his experiences in testing soil, the availability of building material, even down to the quality of the water. After weeks of searching to no avail, Mungo and his disciples stopped in a clearing to rest. Leading them in prayer, Mungo asked the Lord for a divine sign, as he was becoming weary of foot trying to find the right place.

From the woods came a huge wild boar and, as if to challenge them, it rushed up to Mungo, stopped in front of him, stamped its trotters on the ground, then turned and ran back to the edge of the forest. The entire group watched in amazement as the boar repeated this ritual a few more times. The final time that the boar ran to the forest edge and waited, Mungo remembered that the Lord had in times before used animals to guide him. He called on his disciples to follow the boar through the forest, and they did so until they came out on the other side. Before them stretched a wonderful landscape. The boar ran forward, dipped its head and scratched the ground with its tusks, so marking the spot the Lord had ordained as the place Mungo should build his new monastery. This done, to the wonderment of his disciples, the boar came right up to Mungo's feet and, as if in honour, it bowed its head to him.

'The Lord will bless you for carrying out His will in guiding me to this chosen spot,' Mungo said, blessing the boar. With its task over, the boar turned and disappeared into the forest, back to where it came from. Mungo walked into the middle of the clearing and planted a cross; this cross had been lovingly cut and carried all the way, prepared for such a day as this. All this he found to his liking on the banks of the River Elwy, in the Vale of Clwyd.

Setting about building the monastery to Mungo's specifications, they worked tirelessly and soon a wonderful creation started to rise from the ground. The Lord had chosen a good place, as the harvest of good souls in this area was mostly Christian. In no time word spread among the faithful, and the good people flocked to this place, drawn by the Lord to Mungo. The first priority he allotted to the people was to clear the land around for farming. Having seen the way the monastery of David had been built, Mungo split his helpers into three groups: the first group was to prepare the land, the second to help in the building of the monastery, and the last group to fetch the material for the building. Over the weeks and months, the building grew tall and straight on the plan Mungo had set out.

Word reached the ears of a certain pagan bandit prince of the area, named Melconde Galganu. Riding with his soldiers and camp scavengers, they rode into the clearing where Mungo's monastery was taking shape. Having been challenged to explain what right he had to build in this place, Mungo told Prince Melconde that it was on the authority of his own lord, King Cathwallian, that he build this monastery to the glory of the Lord. This was not good enough for Melconde, as he hoped one day to become the king, by force if need be. To send out a message over the land, he scattered Mungo's followers and ordered his men to pull to the ground that which had been built. Their deed done, Melconde scorned Mungo and blasphemed the Lord as they rode off.

Not too far down the road, Melconde started to lose his vision. Ordering his men to halt, he called for his healer to rectify the strange affliction that had struck him down. It was to no avail. The veil covering his eyes only grew darker, until finally all was dark. Lost and with nowhere to go, his healer told him that she had heard that the monk called Mungo was a wonderful healer. Melconde ordered his men to take him back to this monk, for he knew that before long his leadership would be taken if he could not regain his sight.

Mungo had gathered back some of his disciples, and had started to clear the site for rebuilding, when suddenly the noise of horses could be heard coming their way. Fearing the worst, most of the monks scattered back into the woods; the few that remained vowed to stand their ground come what may. They could see Melconde riding at the front of the group, albeit being led.

Stopping in front of Mungo, the prince called out in anguish, 'Priest, I have come down with a curse of blindness and I am in need of your healing power. Do this thing and I will spare your people.'

Mungo noted that he did not say he would leave them alone; even so, it was not Mungo's way to turn away from a cry of despair. Rather than hold Melconde's evil deeds against him, he, with the Lord's blessing, would always use good deeds to overcome the evil in man. He told the prince to dismount from his horse, and once he was on the ground Mungo prayed to the Lord. Covering the man's eyes with his hands, he asked the Lord to restore his sight, even though he might persecute the Christians.

The Lord in his magnificence answered Mungo's prayers and restored the prince's sight. As his sight came flooding back the prince saw everything in a clearer light; he knew what he had to do from this day on. He dropped to his knees in front of Mungo and swore, 'From this day on I will follow you and your Lord till my breath leaves my body. My sword and my shield will fight to protect you for the glory of your Lord. All my wealth and possessions are yours to do with what you will for the glory of the Lord who in His benevolence has done this wonderful thing.'

Mungo baptised the prince and his men into the Christian faith. Many of these men took up the cloth, along with the prince. In this hallowed spot, peace descended.

Once again the Lord had turned the darkness into the light, turning wicked men from their evil ways towards a more rewarding way of life, a life of helping their fellow men instead of persecuting them. All this was done by the Lord to show the people that his beloved Mungo was a chosen son of the Almighty, and that while they walked in the light of his teachings no ill would befall them.

While the building was taking place, the great, the noble and the ordinary folk brought their children to the church. Among them was a young man by the name of Asaph, who was to be enrolled into the faithful following of the man they called Kentigern – we shall hear more of him later.

Right from the beginning, the Lord knew how things would be. He had told Mungo that from this spot the faith would surge like the tide over the lands, for this was a special place to Him. In no time at all, Mungo's following had swelled with good men who had forsaken their old lives to serve the Lord under his guidance. It is said that nearly 900 men were the count. Mungo set about arranging his fellow followers. One third of the men, who had very little education, he set the task of tending the fields. One third of the men he gave the special job of tending to the monastery buildings. The last third, being more knowledgeable and learned, he charged to stay within the enclosures of the sanctuary to study the Scriptures and to observe the celebration of the religious services by day and night in all due reverence to the Lord.

In future times, some of these most trusted and learned monks would be allowed out of the enclosure to accompany Mungo on his many missions to covert those souls who were still wandering lost in the wilderness, crying out for someone to guide them to the Lord and Saviour. Soon, for them, the darkness that had filled their lives would be lifted and a new dawn would begin.

It must have been a very welcome event for Saint Mungo to be greeted by someone of like mind, like Saint David. Both had the same drive and the same belief in the way that the gospel should be preached. The monastery David built was the largest of its time. It is unknown what materials he used, but as the Romans had been in that region a long time and other buildings have been excavated that were built of stone, it is possible that the first monastery could have been built using both wood and stone. Today a cathedral stands in the same spot.

Legend has it that Saint Mungo converted Merlin near Drumelzier, west of Peebles. A theory of mine is that the legendary Merlin and Saint Mungo were in all probability the same person. Saint Mungo was a worker of miracles not magical tricks; Merlin is reputed to have performed magic. Is it possible that Arthur, a Christian king, would seek out a Druid when he had a man of God who performed miracles in the name of the Lord, and was his confidant? Further proof may be found in the timing of the stories regarding Saint Mungo and Merlin. Saint Mungo's life stories were first recorded around the tenth century, while the stories linking Merlin to him appear around the fifteenth century. There are similarities between some of the stories, which you can read in the following chapters.

Mungo's Prodigy, Asaph

Many long months after the hard work of building the new monastery and church, Mungo and his followers stood in front of the newly consecrated altar in the chapel of the completed monastery, praising the Lord by offering up the first of many masses to the Almighty God for all the benevolence and guidance He had given them over the building, this wonderful house for the worship of He who is the one true God. The interior of the chapel was beautifully prepared by craftsmen whose hands had been guided by the Lord; the tabernacle was carved out of the finest oak and stained with a gold dye. It shone as the sunlight beamed upon this most holy place. That day there wasn't enough room inside for all those who had attended this solemn dedication.

With his work to build the monastery completed, Mungo turned his mind to the real task the Lord had destined him for. There were still men and women who were ignorant of the Lord's way; they had led lives of paganism for far too long. Mungo could hear the souls call out for redemption from many who were lost. He knew his work would never be done until the whole land and the people were singing the praises of the Almighty Lord, who is the life of all creation, the light that is the only way to reach the house of God in heaven. So to the learned monks who had accompanied him from Saint David's, he gave instructions to teach the new disciples in the ways that the Lord had laid down in Scripture. Obedience to the Lord in everything they do, he told them, was the most important lesson. 'Abstinence from overindulging,' he instructed them, 'is the true way of penance. Be servants of the people and love your brothers as Christ loves us.'

When he had settled all his disciples in the places most suited to their skills, Mungo felt he could take time out for quiet prayer. Then the Lord called him to renew his mission, to seek out and spread the word, he took himself off to a place of solitude to listen to the Lord's instruction in preparation. His disciples would come to know this was the way of a saint.

Mungo returned to his church on the eve of Easter Sunday, having spent weeks living rough, eating only the roots of the wild plants and drinking rainwater. Fasting was his way of cleansing his soul to enable him to be pure in the eyes of the Lord, so that he could participate in the taking of the body and blood of the Lord with a pure soul on this holiest of days. This day He would strengthen and renew his faith in the Light of the risen Lord, whose death on the cross promised that he who is not unworthy but believes will be reborn, unstained with the sins of the times. This the Lord had promised.

Mungo was greeted by his joyful followers, who had all waited in anticipation of his return. This was the time of year when all the Church was united as one in the praise of the Lord Jesus Christ. For future missions, Mungo selected a few of his most ready of monks to travel with him, telling them to take only their Bibles and the clothes they were wearing. 'The Lord will provide,' he always told them, and the Lord had not let his chosen son down on his missions in the past. His missions took them to places that had not heard the word of Jesus; these souls he confirmed into the faith. In areas where saints had before laid down the faith, he strengthened it; where they had monks or priests in residence, he instructed them in the way the teachings should be. But as he proceeded, Mungo grew frustrated by the heretics and the many different interpretations laid down by some of the clergy in the areas where the faith had been established. He believed that united teachings were what the Lord commanded of His people.

Each time he returned to his beloved monastery, Mungo felt that this was the only place where he was at peace within himself. Throwing himself into finding a solution to the unification of the teachings, Mungo called together all his most learned disciples and asked them to ponder the matter.

'Only the Seat of Peter has the answer,' he was told. But the Seat of Peter was a long way off in Rome.

'If it is the Lord's will, then so be it,' Mungo told them. He would go to see the Holy Father, the Bishop of Christ, and lay bare his soul and his shortcomings on the teachings of the Word. This would have been a momentous undertaking at any time, but in those days there were only basic forms of transport. None of this mattered to Mungo; this was the will of the Lord.

How long he was away and what way he went is open to conjecture. Suffice to say, he completed the journey on more than one occasion. There are no recordings of his epic journeys, but it is said that when he returned he brought back with him many books of Scripture, as laid down by the Holy See. He also brought back relics of great saints, along with ornaments to adorn the altar of the monastery church. The only part of the route for which we have evidence is that via Koln in Germanium (Germany).

Koln Cathedral

A portrait of Saint Mungo can be seen on one of the pillars in the cathedral, and is the only portrait to survive inside that predates the Reformation. To have this dedication in a land so far away, we can only assume he carried out some great miracles whilst there. Laden as he was when he returned home, he was welcomed by a homecoming that was reserved only for the holiest of saints.

Once settled, he set to work preparing his monks and students in the ways the Pontiff had laid down, envisioning that there was only one Church and all must be united in the one Holy Catholic Christian faith.

When on his rounds, Mungo sought out the youth Asaph. The bond between them had grown ever since the young Asaph had been enrolled into the monastery school, as Mungo had seen the light of the Lord in this student's eyes; a gentleness and beauty that only the Lord in His divine wisdom could have bestowed. Mungo nurtured his innocence the way his own mentor, Servanus, had done for him. Asaph had shown in many small ways that the Lord had touched him and bestowed his blessings on him, and this Mungo wanted to see burst forth in all its glory in praise of the Lord's name.

Years of long hard devotion to the Lord were beginning to age Mungo; he was now in his early fifties and not enthusiastic to go out as much. His mind was willing, but the ravages of age were weakening his body. This the Lord could see, and He let Mungo know that He had given him all His blessings and could take them all away. One day, in the dead of winter, Mungo washed himself in the manner he had always done, by submerging himself in the stream nearby. But this morning, unlike other times, something strange happened to him. The Lord had always dried him even as he lifted up out of the water, but today when he stepped from the water he felt a cold he had never experienced in all his life. The Lord was punishing his beloved son for his disobedience and laziness in not pursuing his mission as vigorously as He had willed. Mungo felt cold and shivery and his bones ached. It was an illness of which he had no understanding.

He returned to his cell in the monastery and called on the saintly boy, Asaph. He impressed on him that he was in need of warmth because the Lord had inflicted on him a cold such as he had never known. The young Asaph hurried down to the kitchen and implored the cook to give him some live coals so that he may warm up Mungo, his master. The cook told him, 'Take all you need, but I have nothing to give that you may carry them in. If you so desire them for your master, you will need to hold out your habit to carry them in.'

As it was his master's dearest wish for some heat to warm his aching bones, Asaph, praying to the Lord, picked up the live coals and placed them in his habit. He hurried back and, arriving in Mungo's cell, dropped the live coals on the floor at the bishop's feet. Looking at Asaph's habit, Mungo could not see any scorch or burn marks. The Lord had indeed looked with favour on this gentle and obedient boy. Mungo praised the Lord for having shown him the errors of his ways and for revealing the one to whom He had chosen to bestow blessings on. From that moment Mungo felt the warmth glow within his body and all the aches and pains that had afflicted him lifted away.

As the years passed, every day, with the love of Jesus and the fire of his faith, Mungo burned away the evils of the past, kindling the flame of hope in the hearts and souls of all those whom he had baptised into the family of the Lord. Many miracles, it is said, were performed by Mungo and by some of his devoted monks during this time. Asaph grew in stature and, like Mungo in youth, he was a dedicated student of all the Scriptures. As soon as it was permitted in age, Mungo ordained Asaph. With Asaph's knowledge and understanding of all things, it was not long before he was rewarded with a higher position within the monastery. It would have looked to the casual observer as if Mungo, with the guidance of the Lord, was training a successor to take his place.

With Asaph now directing the way ahead for the monastery, Mungo found a new vigour and was gone for longer periods at a time doing the Lord's work. Sometimes his travels would take him into virgin territory where the pagan influence was strong. The courage the Lord had bestowed on him held him in good stead, for while the pagan chiefs challenged Mungo they were no match for the word of the Lord as spoken by Mungo. The apostle of Jesus spread the good word and changed the land with the word; the Lord Jesus Christ's name was known and revered by all that first heard the word from Saint Mungo.

One day, on one of his missions, he had a vision of a great

battle which would take place in the not-too-distant future. His anguish at the slaughter he saw made him kneel down and pray for the souls of those who would lose their lives, especially those who had not accepted the Christian faith.

Back at the monastery, Mungo submerged himself in his devotions to the Lord. He always felt pleased to be able to attend the solemn services of the divine sacraments in his beloved monastery. His following had increased even though many had gone out into the world to follow the calling of the Lord. Many who wanted to serve the Lord followed the road to the monastery, but few were chosen. Those who did not or could not follow the hard monastic life set up home near the monastery. In time, a township would grow up around the monastery and be named after the saint who took over the leadership of the monastic life. It would in future be known in Welsh as Llanelwy and in English as the town of Saint Asaph.

As it came to pass, Mungo heard one day that the great battle he had dreamt of had taken place back in his beloved land of Cambria. The Lord had shown him in his vision that it was time for a renewal of the Christian faith in the Cambrian kingdom. On the Lord's instructions, Mungo had prepared everyone and everything around the monastery that was needed. The Lord was well pleased with his most devoted and obedient son whose rewards would be great in heaven. But for now, the Lord had more missions for Mungo to complete.

Not much that was recorded around that time has survived, and it is not until around the eleventh century, in Jocelyn's book, that the foundation of Mungo's magnificent monastery is first recorded. In the present-day cathedral dedicated to Saint Asaph, there is a magnificent stained-glass windows illustrating and dedicated to our beloved Saint Mungo (under his other name, Saint Kentigern). There is another window of Saint Asaph. There are no known dedications to Saint Mungo in this area other than the window. It is thought that as the influence of Saint Mungo waned with his leaving, Saint Asaph took over the minds and hearts of the people. This may have been the reason for the change in dedication. As with Glasgow the influence of Saint

Mungo lingered on in the town long after he left. The town of Saint Asaph grew and became a most important centre of religious life and commerce.

Of Saint Mungo's journeys to Rome to meet with the popes of that time, only from the book *Vita Kentigerni*, written by the monk Jocelyn, that we get an insight into these epic travels of Saint Mungo. It is said Saint Mungo made seven trips to Rome. These journeys must have taken him fully six months at least to complete.

The Battle of Ardderyd

The air was still and the sea fog spread over the land around the River Esk, making it very difficult to see. The sounds that could be heard were from the marching of feet, the neighing of horses and the rattle of steel. The pagan king, Cynfarch Oer, had held these lands for nearly twenty years with brutal force, but in the year AD 573 the time of his reckoning was near. With his army of cut-throats, he stood waiting in this field to meet his new foes. He had held the people of Cambria under the heel of oppression, and now he faced the biggest challenge to his reign. The army he was about to face was much more than an army of trained fighting men – it was an uprising of Christian peasants. He and his men had been fighting this growing army for months and had been pushed back to this place. This was an army with right on its side and the Lord God as its champion. The army was led by the Christian king, Rydderck Hael, son of the late King Elidyr of the Britons, and assisted by Aidan, the future king of Scotic Dalriada.

King Rydderck had for the last few years been gathering an army loyal to the cross, and had once again established himself in the ancient fortification of his father, Alcluid. He had also cemented an alliance with his good friend, Aidan, who had been baptised into the faith by Abbot Columba. These two different armies had come together in one common goal, to rid the land of the heathens and relight the flame of Christianity. It was Columba who Rydderck turned to for counselling in the absence of a councillor of the holy order nearer home. Before planning the battle, Rydderck asked Columba if he would lose his life to the heathen enemies in combat. Columba told him not to fret over this, as the Lord would be by his side and he would die on his own bed.

Skirmish after skirmish they fought wherever they found the enemy, ridding the land of the evil stench that the soil had

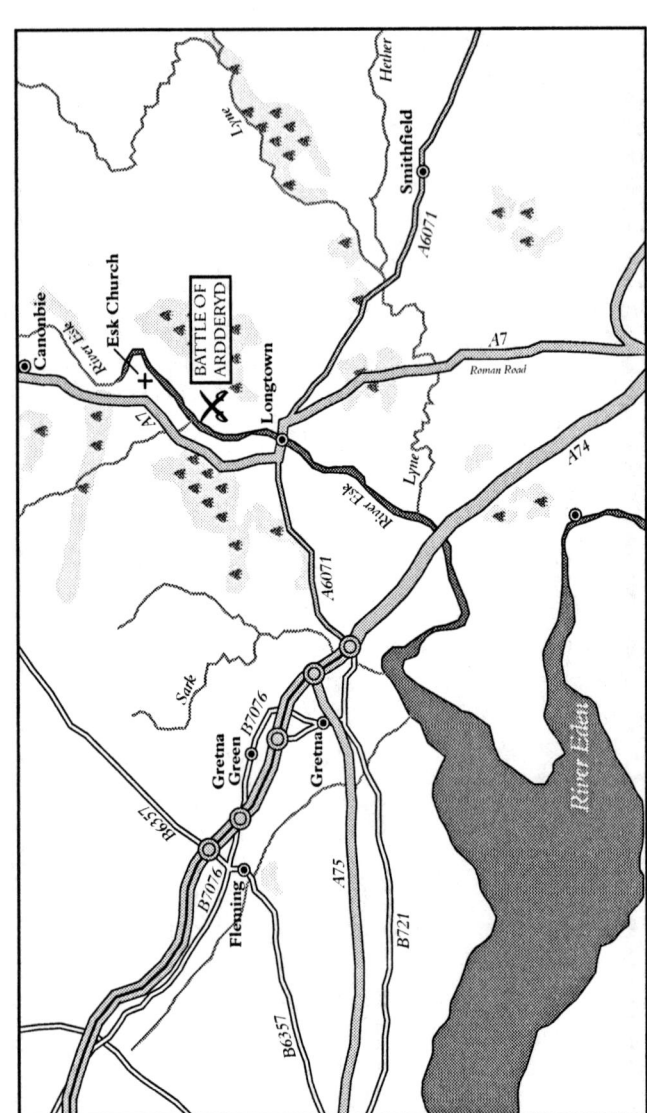

The Battle of Ardderyd (Arthuret) took place eight miles north of Carlisle on the River Esk near the modern-day town of Longtown

absorbed. As they fought their way south, the people rejoiced in their newfound freedom. Even though twenty years had passed since their beloved Mungo had left, the seeds of hope he had sown were waiting to spring. But the grip of the Druids would not easily be broken. Rydderck knew this, although he did not have the time or the know-how to re-establish the Christian faith. That was a task for someone still loved by the people of the only area to retain their beliefs, a place where he himself had found the strength that had given him the will to take up the sword and become a soldier in the name of the Lord who is most high. For the moment, that task of rekindling the faith would have to be carried out by the loyal monks of the order that the beloved Mungo had set up. This he had told the elders of Glashgu: 'Go out and prepare the people for the day I have prayed for, the return of our one beloved saint, who, above all, was ordained to spread the gospel of the Lord.'

On this cold, misty morning, the heathen armies, under the leadership of Cynfarch Oer, had been backed into a corner. For them it was a fight to the death, with no quarter given; with their backs to the river, the heathens were trapped with nowhere to run. So their leader decided to make his stand in this place, known as Ardderyd (Arthuret) eight miles north of present-day Carlisle. It was an area of deserted moorland split by the fast flowing River Esk, and surrounded by forest. The fog that day took a while to lift. For hours both camps sized up the opposition, each side taunting the other with insults – a tactic to draw the weaker-willed into battle before they were ready.

Small skirmishes broke out, but by midday the sun began to shine from behind the Christian armies, burning away the fog. This is what Rydderck had been waiting for. Before sending his men into battle, he stood before them and bellowed, 'For too long you have suffered oppression under this heathen king, but you will no longer be oppressed. Today with your Lord's help your victory will be the start of a new freedom, a freedom of peace. You fight today for a just cause with the Almighty Lord on your side. You fight for the glory of your faith, Christianity.'

With trumpets blowing, he ordered the first charge on the heathen army. Running down the slope, yelling like wild dogs, they charged into the fray. When the armies clashed, the sound could be heard all over the province. At the front of the first wave was Rydderck, as brave a king that ever walked this land. The fighting was bloody and ferocious; no one that fell would ever again stand in the sunlight of life. As the battle progressed for what seemed like hours, it looked for a time that Rydderck's men were being pushed back, but this was a tactical move so that the army of King Aidan could swoop round and attack from both sides at once.

Surrounded on three sides with the river blocking their retreat, and with the battle now reaching a bloodier stage, the heathens fought like demons possessed, with every dirty trick they could muster. All this time Cynfarch Oer had kept himself out of harm's way. Now, though, he would have to draw his sword and fight, and fight he did – with the fierceness of a man who has had to fight all his days to maintain his power in the kingdom.

As the battle wore on it was destined that the two kings should meet face to face; this was how the Lord had planned it. One was the champion of the Lord, the other the Devil's defender of evil. It was a titanic struggle, with both men giving their all until the sword of the cross pierced the armour of the Devil. Cynfarch dropped to his knees. Staring up with surprise at Rydderck, he opened his mouth to breathe his last. Falling on his back, looking up, the last thing he saw before being dispatched to meet the Devil whose ways he had cherished so much was a single white dove fluttering over the battlefield.

It took some time for the news to spread across the field that the tyrant had been slain and that victory was won in the name of the Lord Jesus Christ. When the realisation struck home to the heathen soldiers left standing that all was lost, to a man they threw down their weapons and asked for mercy. With victory won, Rydderck was feeling generous. He granted them amnesty and ordered them never again to take up arms against the Christian people. Surveying the battlefield and all the dead lying there, the two kings who had come through unscathed knelt down and said prayers of thanksgiving for their victory. It was a day that would be remembered by all, a day on which Christians came together in unity to fight for the right to practise their faith without persecution.

On the long march home many happy people came out to greet their heroes. As was the fashion in those days, flowers were thrown in front of the king's horses. Wherever a Christian population of size was, the priest (who, usually, had suffered the most under the oppression) came out and offered holy mass up for the praising of the Lord's name. All the way home Rydderck saw a need for the re-evangelising of the Christian faith, and this he swore would be his first priority. Once home and after all the celebrations, he called together all his wise men of council.

'How should I proceed in the restoration of the Christian faith throughout the land?' he asked.

There was much grunting and groaning, but no answers were forthcoming. With disappointment written all over his face the King dismissed them all, telling them he would have had better advice from the knaves in the streets.

That night the thought came to him, as if planted mystically in his head, that he should go to Glashgu. There he would find the answers to his quest, as there could be found the monks who still kept in touch with their teacher and mentor, Mungo. Early next day he set off with his escort to Glashgu to seek the council of the monks.

Even after Mungo had left on his mission Glashgu had grown even larger, and the sizeable town was still growing around the Molendinar Burn. Smaller settlements had sprung up within a short distance of the main settlement making this area, as it is today, one of the most populated areas in Scotland. Arriving at the expanding ecclesiastical centre that was now dedicated to their beloved founder, Mungo, the King was pleased with the work being carried out from this centre.

Gathered together, the monks with one voice called on the King to send an envoy down to plead with Mungo, nay, to order Mungo to return with all speed. The completion of Christianity of the whole kingdom of Cambria was in need of his mission and the people were crying out once more for his divine leadership to guide them into the world before them. Only he who was the chosen son of the Lord could fulfil all this for the glory in the

Lord's name, who is the one Almighty God. Hearing his subjects, the King put together a company of his most learned people and priests, and with all the people's heartfelt pleas ringing in their ears for Mungo's return, he sent them on their way south.

Academics have placed the Battle of Ardderyd (Arthuret) as having taken place approximately eight miles north of Carlisle near the River Esk. This would place the battle near the town of Longtown on the A7 road. This battle is probably the first time an army fought under a Christian banner in this country.

The Journey Home

In the year AD 574, on a bright spring morning, the Lord sent a celestial messenger to Mungo in the form of a wispy cloud. This cloud descended down until it came to rest in front of him. Within it, Mungo could see a group of travellers heading his way. A voice from the cloud told him that these men had come all the way from his past home, Glashgu. Their mission was to beseech Mungo to return home to be their spiritual head once again and to lead them to fulfil the promise he had made years before of building a Christian nation once more in Ystrat Clud. The voice from the cloud said, 'My beloved son, I, your Lord, am pleased with all you have done for Me, but now it is time for you to return home to where the people will honour you above all men to the glory of My name.'

When the vision of the cloud disappeared, Mungo knew it would be a wrench to leave this home, where he had found a peace he had not known before. He had long since harboured the hope of spending his last few days in the monastery he loved; he had worked long and hard to erect the place to the glory of the Lord. But he knew in his heart that the Lord had not put him here on earth to enjoy an easy life. Mungo also knew that the Lord's will would be done, no matter what his own feelings were. He, after all, was nothing without the Lord and his life and services were for the Lord to do with as He willed. Leaving all his beloved followers would be sad but he knew their hearts would be filled with a new love for his most devoted follower, Asaph. With his heart heavy, he called together all his people and told them of the vision he had had from the Lord and of the consequences, even before the emissaries had arrived. He told them all he would be leaving this place and that he would be charging his most devoted servant, Asaph, whom God had found favour in, to take over the running of the monastery and ecclesiastical life.

'Follow him from this day on and listen to his words,' he said, 'for they are not his own but those of the Almighty who is your Father in heaven.'

A few days later the deputation from Glashgu arrived and Mungo met with his old friends. Learning of all that had gone on since he had left, Mungo was pleased that the church he had founded was still thriving. He was not so pleased, however, to hear of all the idolatry and debauchery being practised in the name of Satan over the rest of the land. This, he told them, the Lord had commanded him to set to rights.

When the farewells were done and preparations made for leaving, a farewell mass of dedication to their most holy man's work in the area and for his future life was said. For the last time, Mungo offered up the Holy Sacraments in thanksgiving in the monastery church that had been built with the help and the blessings of the Lord. When mass was over, for the last time, Mungo left the monastery church by the north door in the procession. It is said that from that day on, the north door of the church is opened for one day each year to commemorate their love for Mungo and the hope that, even if only in spirit, he may return.

Nearly 300 of Mungo's faithful followers, mostly of Welsh descent, who had been schooled by him on the Scriptures went with him. They would be of a great assistance to Mungo in the coming years. The emissaries had gone ahead to prepare the King for his return. The road taken by the saint took them back through familiar territory. Stopping for a time at Karleolum (Carlisle) to speak with the bishop of that day and finding that the clergy had been neglecting their duty to the people in the outlying areas, Mungo left some of his own followers to correct the wrongdoing.

Proceeding on his journey, he was finally met by Rydderck and a multitude of people at a place called Hodelm (Hoddom Cross).

Here some heard Mungo for the first time and were in awe. He lectured them on the evils of the pagan way of life and this time they were in no doubt as to what was needed to follow the Christian faith. In his book, Jocelyn professed to quote Saint

Mungo as he preached to the multitude, saying, of the pagans, 'Their idols were the vain inventions of men, more fitted for the fire than for worship. The elements of nature which they invoked were the creations of the Maker adapted for the use of men; and Woden, whose worship the Angles had introduced among them, was only a pagan mortal, though a Saxon king, whose body was turned to dust.' After that, he preached to them the faith that is in Jesus Christ, and the sacraments of faith.

Mungo decided to make Hodelm his base; from here he would spread the faith. A Celtic cross was planted on the spot, which became known as Hodelm Cross. A church was built to serve the faithful who were scattered over a wide area. (The foundations of a sixth-century church have been found there in recent times.)

Travelling into Dumfries and Galloway, Mungo rekindled the Christian faith. This was a more difficult job than at first thought: over the neglected years the influx of Anglian heathens had enforced their paganism on the people, even to the point of death.

Saint Mungo's mission took him into an area known as 'The Machars'. Here it is said he settled for a while in a cave at Whithorn that was the ancient home of Saint Ninian at Whithorn. The restoration of the faith in Saint Ninian's land gave Saint Mungo great joy, to see that once again the Lord's name would be praised in this earliest of settlements. Saint Mungo's episcopate work was never-ending, but through his efforts and with the blessings of the Lord, he did restore the Christian faith over the area, and dedicated his efforts to the memory of the blessed son of God, Saint Ninian.

His dilemma over how to stop the idolatry and paganism that had spread throughout the rest of the Cambrian kingdom was causing Saint Mungo a lot of pain. Asking the Lord for guidance did not lead to an easy solution. In his prayers, the Lord had answered him by saying, 'Seek out the one whom is the Bishop of all bishops on earth. He is wise and has found great favour with Me.'

Saint Mungo, having spent the best part of three years in the Galloway area turning back the tide of heathenism, did not cherish this journey. To go to Rome in his sixtieth year was a journey that would be more of a penance. Calling around him all his ordained followers, he explained that he had to make a trip to Rome before returning to his beloved Glashgu. Leaving some to carry on with the mission he had started, all but a few of the remainder he told to travel to Glashgu and prepare for his homecoming.

The journey of Saint Mungo and his followers was long and arduous but in time they arrived in Rome to find out that the pope of that day was Pope Benedictus I. He was a holy man and was truly blessed by the Lord Almighty. It was he who would start the Roman Catholic faith on the right path that the Lord had willed. Saint Mungo had many audiences with Pope Benedictus, and on one occasion he laid bare his soul, telling of his feelings of not being in a position of authority to carry out the Lord's will. On hearing Mungo's woes, Pope Benedictus, having been guided by the Lord, confirmed to Saint Mungo that the Almighty Himself, having received the apostolic blessings and absolution, blessed his election and consecration to high order of bishop. Fortified by a new inner resolve received from Pope Benedictus, after a time Saint Mungo began planning to return home, in the knowledge of faith shown in him by the Holy Father. As a parting gift, Pope Benedictus gave Saint Mungo some relics of past saints and some ornaments to adorn the altar of his beloved church in Glashgu. One other gift he received from the pontiff was a clear direction of how the church should travel so that the people would know that Christ's blessings are on those who follow his teachings.

On the long journey home, it is not known which direction he took. It is assumed that because of his links with the city of Koln in Germany, he would have used this way again. Koln was one of the major places of pilgrimage as the relics of the Magi lay there. Arriving back on his homeland soil, word spread fast over the kingdom. In anticipation for the homecoming of their beloved bishop plans were set down for a great celebration throughout the land. The King had organised an entourage to travel down the road to meet and escort Saint Mungo home in the manner fitting one who is loved by the Almighty Lord above all earthly men.

Saint Kentigern (Mungo), painted on a pillar in the chapel of Saint Stephan, Cologne (Köln) Cathedral.

The year was AD 578. Saint Mungo had now spent sixty-one years on this earth, all in the service of the Lord. Unlike many monks of that time, Saint Mungo had abstained from alcohol, meat and the pleasures of the flesh, preferring as he had all his life to devote himself only to the Lord's mission and to serve the children of the faith, with no blemish of sin. Saint Mungo still walked in a manner more suited to a much younger man and was, for his age, still very fit. The distances he had to cover on foot in his duties to carry out the Lord's will and the places to which he travelled are truly mind-boggling. His epic journeys are not written down in any great books, but only in the fables passed down by generations of believers. But one thing we can be sure of is that it was all carried out through his great love for the Lord. He also knew that his new mission to rebuild the fabric of this society that had been for so long in the dark would need all his best efforts and the blessings of the Lord.

When they arrived home in around AD 579, the welcome awaiting Mungo and his small band of followers on the outskirts of Glashgu was greater than their wildest dreams. The people's tears of joy washed the streets clean – their holy bishop was home. Entering the town, the monks who were with Saint Mungo started ringing hand-held bells of peace that they had carried all the way from the Holy Father Benedictus. These were gifts to this great nation as one of the chosen children of the Lord. The bells rang out a new message to the people and lifted up their voices in the praising of the Lord. Glashgu was once again the centre of holiness, which would send out the rays of hope and burn all the old ways of idolatry from the land.

Up into the centre of the town they went, with crowds thronging all around. People lifted their children up for the saints to bless, believing that even the shadow of Saint Mungo would absolve them of their sins. With tears of love welling up in his eyes, Saint Mungo said a silent prayer: 'Lord, this is surely why you have brought me back home to my beloved Glashgu. Praised be your name for having brought me home. May I, with your blessing, win over the hearts and souls of this great land to the glory of your name.'

The crowds eagerly ushered the entourage forward, right into the square in front of the now enlarged church that Saint Mungo had started so many years before.

Rydderck, his queen, Languoreth, and all his family had travelled over from his fortress Alcluid to be there on that special day. The King, who had been a young boy when he had first seen Saint Mungo, remembered how his father loved this holy man for his wise counsel. He also remembered all the tales of the miracles he had performed, and his unfailing duty to the Almighty Lord and his service to his people. This was the day he had been looking forward to for a great number of years, what he had been fighting for, what that bloody day at Ardderyd had been fought for when all those lives were given up in the name of Christianity: the hope of the day when they would have their own Lord's bishop to show them the true way to the Lord Jesus.

When he saw Saint Mungo on this occasion, he noticed the glow of inner holiness that surrounded him. Saint Mungo stood in the centre of the square and blessed and thanked all the people for their warm welcome. At that, as if the Lord was moving his feet, the King moved forward and knelt down in front of Saint Mungo as his father had done all those years before, showing to his subjects that even a king kneels before a holy man of God. As Saint Mungo raised his hand to the heavens, the people all knelt down.

Saint Mungo placed one hand on the King's head and said in prayer, 'Lord bless this man, Your faithful servant, for all the things he has done in Your name. Forgive him for his human failings. With Your help and by his own hand, Lord, he has smote Your enemies and rid the land of those evildoers who worshipped false idols and would desecrate Your name. Give him the wisdom of Solomon so that from this day on he will rule his kingdom with love and fairness in Your name.' Pausing, in silent prayer he then continued, 'Lord, in Your magnificence hear the plea of the people: give them the will to follow Your Commandments and live as You would have them do. Bless the land with all their needs and, Lord, in Your mercy, let Glashgu flourish by the praising of Your name and the preaching of Your word.'

At this it is said in folklore that the ground under Saint

Mungo's feet rose up, lifting him on a high mound so that all present could see and have no doubts that this was a true saint chosen by the Lord God.

The motto of Glasgow is 'Let Glasgow Flourish'. It is said to have been taken from Saint Mungo's speech when he arrived back in his beloved Glashgu. Glasgow, as we all know, has indeed flourished into one of the most vibrant cities in the world. If only the people could show the same faith in the Lord as Saint Mungo did, the city of Glasgow could well go on to become once again the centre of religious excellence.

Eighteenth-century coat of arms

The Ring of Truth

Over the next few years Saint Mungo travelled far and wide around the kingdom, visiting and setting up as many parishes as he could. In these years there was a good harvest of souls for the Lord. Peace had settled over the land, and prosperity was blooming. With the huge number of monks Saint Mungo had returned to Glashgu with, he was able to establish and build churches all over the land. For once, all the people sang the same praises of the Lord.

To the north of the kingdom in the lands of the Picts, Christianity was making inroads into pagan society, driven by the soldier of the Lord who one day would be known as Saint Columba. Saint Columba had for some time heard of the man called Mungo who performed many miracles in the name of the Lord, and he vowed that one day, the Lord permitting, he would travel to meet with this great man of God. But his work, like that of Saint Mungo's, kept that day far off.

Back in Glashgu, Saint Mungo had his followers build a small abode for him a place where he could retreat to when in the need of solitude for prayer. As the years took their toll on his mind and body, his time away on his missions grew shorter. His faithful followers were always glad when he stayed among them to preach the Scriptures. Around the year AD 584, in his sixty-sixth year, Saint Mungo was brought to a sudden halt as the Lord reminded him of his purpose in this life; retirement was not on the agenda. One night in his restless sleep, the Lord sent an angel to tell him to awake and prepare for one last mission in his name. This mission was to return to the land north of his birth, which was in need of his tongue to convert the heathen lands there.

On the next morning, Mungo gathered some of his most loyal disciples together who had been with him through all the days he had been in Wales. He told them of the Lord pressing on him the need to chase the demons of idolatry from the land known as

Fortriu, (Angus and Aberdeenshire), one of the northern Pictish kingdoms. In all probability, with the map of Scotland at that time Saint Mungo may have retraced his steps back the way he had come. In doing so he would have crossed over the Forth at the same point he crossed before, near Athluath (Alloa) and in that way would have strengthened his ties with this area and a dedication to him would have been more likely. His mission would have taken him back into parts of Fife, from where he could have followed the old Roman road over the Ochil Hills to Dunning and on to a river crossing near Perth, before heading right up into the upper Dee Valley.

His labour was rewarded with many converts and the establishing of many churches over the area. Most churches dedicated to Saint Mungo have an unmistakable Welsh name, such as Glengairden. Others are Migvie, Llanfinan or Finan, and Midmar dedicated to Nidan, one of Saint Mungo's disciples. Two parishes in Anglesea in Wales have dedications to two saints, Llanfinan and Llannidan. It is believed they worked alongside Saint Mungo, both here and in Wales. Saint Mungo spent a considerable time in this area establishing new parishes and his work did not go unnoticed during the time he was there, for there is an old Aberdonian saying, 'Saint Mungo's werk is ne'er dun'.

Returning to Glashgu in his seventieth year to a tremendous welcome, Mungo had left behind on Dee-side some of his disciples to carry on the good work and, in future time, to become saints. Now in Glashgu, he settled back into monastic life, teaching and offering up the sacred solemn mass. But dealing with the everyday running of the diocese of the huge kingdom was beginning to take its toll. Saint Mungo made one of many trips to counsel the King, who had become dependent on his wisdom since he first came back all those years ago. On arriving back at his beloved abode in Glashgu he went into solitude for a while and would not enter into conversation with anyone except the Lord.

When his forced silence had passed, one morning while he was praying in the chapel he was visited by a vision. To the astonishment of those around him, his face took on a brilliant glow of white light, as though on fire. Transfixed by this, they could only look on in awe. The light that shone from Saint Mungo's face was like a glimpse of heaven; never had they seen anything so wondrous before. Saint Mungo slumped to the floor and cried profusely, unable to hold back the tears. After a while, the vision passed and he related to those present that he had seen the soul of Saint David leave his earthly body to be escorted up to heaven, there to be greeted by a great multitude of angels who led him to be with the Lord for ever. (Saint David died in the year AD 589.) Saint Mungo continued, saying, 'A bright light of Our Lord has departed from this world, and it will leave a space that I fear may not be filled for a long time. It was he, Saint David, who stayed the Lord's hand when the Lord wanted to smite the evil men of that region. It was he and he alone, with Your blessings, Oh Lord, who pulled Your people out of the darkness they had been in and brought them into the light of You, Oh Lord. I fear we are going to go through turbulent times for a while, but stay strong and trust in the Lord.'

Some of Saint Mungo's disciples travelled down to Wales to verify the death of the saintly man who was one of the chosen sons of the Lord. It was confirmed that the death of Saint David was indeed on the same hour and minute that Saint Mungo had seen the raising up of his soul into heaven in his vision.

It was not long after this period that Queen Languoreth had an illicit liaison with one of the young knights of the King's court. During one of their meetings, the Queen, after some persuasion, gave to her lover a ring as a keepsake. This ring was a gift she had received from her husband the King. It came to pass that, one day, the King noticed that the Queen was without the ring he had given to her. Having heard the rumours of her affair, but not wanting to admit to himself that it could be true, he decided to trick the Queen. One day he casually asked her to please him for a special occasion by wearing the ring. In a panic, the Queen tried to contact the knight but it was to no avail: the knight was away on the King's business in the realm. When the banquet came round, the Queen appeared in all her splendour, but with a different ring on her finger. The King asked her why she wasn't wearing the ring he had given her. The Queen, embarrassed at the King's enquiry, lied, saying she had misplaced the ring and couldn't find it. For the moment the King decided to leave it and deal with the matter later.

A few weeks later, when hunting with a group of knights, by chance he happened to see the ring in question on the finger of his most trusted knight. Not wanting to cause a fuss at that time, he waited till the hunting party was asleep. He crept over to the knight and slipped the ring from the knight's finger with the intention of challenging them together. His anger though got the better of him, and in a rage he threw the ring into the River Clyde. Kneeling down he prayed, asking forgiveness for his anger. He felt that his feelings for his Queen had betrayed his position as King.

The next day, the Queen asked the knight to return the ring. He declined, saying that he had lost it while out hunting. When the King asked again for the Queen to produce the ring, she locked herself in her room, pleading illness. Calling one of her squires to her chamber, she gave him a note to take to Saint Mungo, whom she felt was the only one who could save her in her disgrace. With all haste, the squire travelled to Glashgu and presented the note to Saint Mungo.

In the note the Queen laid bare her indiscretion and told of the consequences; pouring out her heart, she asked for his forgiveness. She told him she was still in love with her husband the King and would do whatever Saint Mungo asked of her. The holy man pondered the letter and gave much thought to the best way to solve this unholy deed that had struck this good king and his queen. Praying for guidance, in a vision he saw the King remove the ring from the knight's finger and throw it into the river.

Saint Mungo asked the squire if he had ever fished. The squire answered, 'No, Your Holiness.' Saint Mungo gave the squire a fishing rod and said to him, 'Go down to the river and cast in this line. The first fish you pull from the river, with all haste return to me.'

Obeying his bishop, the squire carried out his request, and lo and behold, at the very first cast caught a huge salmon. The salmon gave no trouble; as though by the Lord's command, it swam right into the squire's arms. Running back, he placed the salmon before Saint Mungo. After removing the hook, Saint Mungo put his fingers into the salmon's mouth and withdrew a ring, not any ring, but the self-same ring the King had thrown into the river. The squire was sworn to remain silent on what he had seen. Saint Mungo picked up the salmon and, stroking it, he said, 'You have done all that the Lord has asked of you; go now and swim in peace with the Lord's blessings.' He then released the salmon into the Molendinar Burn, from where it swam down into the river.

Saint Mungo decided to travel with the squire to hand over the ring to the Queen in person. On arrival he made his way straight to her chambers. Confronting her, he asked her why she had let herself and the King down. She confessed all to the holy saint, who absolved her of her sins. Seeing how fraught she was, he then handed to her the ring she had thought would never see the light of day again. Dropping to her knees, she kissed Saint Mungo's hand and swore to stay on the path of righteousness from that day on. Wearing the ring, the Queen, accompanied by Saint Mungo, went into the Great Hall to meet with the King who was in conversation with his knights. At seeing Saint Mungo escorting the Queen, holding high the hand that bore the ring so that all could see, the entire assembly knelt down in homage. The King, as though hypnotised, could not take his eyes of the ring; his thoughts were mixed up.

Did I not take the ring off the knight's finger and throw it into the river? he thought. He had been ready to accuse his queen of adultery in front of the Court. Now he thought he must have been mistaken. Kneeling down in front of the Queen with tears of joy in his eyes, he asked her to forgive him for having doubted her, and, in front of everyone, boldly expressed his love for his Queen.

Saint Mungo later heard from the King of the doubts he had over his Queen's guilt, and of wanting to punish the offenders. Saint Mungo felt the King's pain but knew in his heart that he was a good man. Only when affairs of the heart attack someone does he do irrational things. Saint Mungo told him the Lord was the one and only final judge in earthly sin. Rumours from the wicked will always be around. This, he said, was the fortitude of a king: to forgive those who may hurt all in the name of gossip. To stop further gossip, the King in his wisdom charged the knight who was the centre of all the rumours to take over the protection of his southern border. Thus he removed from the Queen's sight the Devil's temptation that had been put before her.

With his work done, Saint Mungo returned to his beloved community, praising the Lord for all the good things He had bestowed on them. Glashgu continued to flourish and grow; all was good in the kingdom. That was, until Mungo heard that in some places the pagan ritual of lighting the sacrificial Beltane fires to celebrate May Day continued. Enraged at hearing this, Saint Mungo sent out directives to the people, telling them that the festivals of May should only be for the holy Virgin Mother, Mary. He warned the people that the practise of pagan rites must stop or they would suffer the wrath of the Lord's hand.

On the eve of the first night of May, when the fires of Beltane were normally lit, Saint Mungo climbed the small hill behind the

Molendinar Burn to check that his commands had been heeded. On reaching the top he looked to the west, but no fires burned; he looked to the north and the east, again no sign of fires burning. Looking to the south, his heart filled with joy: his people had heard his word and had not lit any fires. From then on, the month of May has been celebrated with reverence for the Holy Mother alone. The bell of the church was made to sound out, calling all to prayer and saying that this day Christianity had finally come home to the Cambrian kingdom.

Here again a story written 500 years before the legend of King Arthur came to light has all the marks of being in part the same story of Arthur, Guinevere and Lancelot. With the true location of the Arthur's kingdom still in doubt, it is possible that the fortress of Alcluid on the Dumbarton Rock was possibly the fabled castle of Camelot.

The fortress of Alcluid (Dunbarton Rock) as it is today.

The Meeting of Saints

Within the kingdom of Cambria, the Church was growing stronger by the day. Saint Mungo's influence was winning over the reluctant pagans; Christianity was now the main religion in the area. To celebrate this, Saint Mungo had a huge cross quarried from a stone block. But the labourers, finding it was too heavy to move (in those days they did not have heavy lifting equipment), let the cross lie where it had been cut. On a Sunday night angels from heaven descended and, uplifting the cross, they carried it to the appointed place, where, with due ceremony they buried it in the ground. That place is now known as the cemetery of the Holy Trinity Church. For many a year after, people suffering with demons and madness were tied to this holy cross and left overnight. In the morning, it is said, all were cured of their demons.

The pagan rituals were still being observed in some stubborn pockets, and these Saint Mungo found very hard to overcome, as some of these superstitions still exist even today. After centuries of obedience to their Druid masters, old habits died hard. The Christians still feared that the old days of persecution would return. It was the influence of Saint Mungo and the teachings of the Lord Jesus Christ that shielded them, but, as it is with people, they never think a good thing will last. To this end, the mission of the Church was to fortify the faith so that, even in adversity, it would survive. For many years Rydderck, under the banner of the Lord, had successfully defended his realm. Weary as he was from constantly repelling would-be invaders, only the counsel from his sons and Saint Mungo had kept his spirits up. His family were also blessed with a sense of responsibility to his subjects; this and his faith were reasons for the stability that existed.

It was about now that the expansion to other centres became the next logical step in the Lord's plan. Saint Mungo, seeing how his beloved Glashgu was developing, decided to establish a religious centre on the south side of the river to enable the parishes there to be better administered. (Recently, an ancient foundation of an old church was found near Govan.) The many men of good will that had arrived at the Molendinar holy centre were welcome additions to Saint Mungo's ever-growing army of workers for the Lord. In time these two areas would come together in the city we know as Glasgow.

Ever since the death of Saint David, Saint Mungo had felt that he had been missing something within his pastoral duties. It was in Easter around the year AD 590 that news filtered through of a new pope who had been installed on the seat of Peter in Rome. Saint Mungo, now nearing his seventy-second year, decided to make one last pilgrimage to see this new leader of the Holy Catholic Church. At this advanced age, it must have been his great devotion to the Lord that made him consider this epic journey. He set off with few companions. There is no way of knowing what way he went, whether by sea or, as has been described before, by foot. Over land, he would have followed the same pilgrims' route. He eventually arrived in Rome, which in those days was in decline, but was still one of the most beautiful cities in the known world.

On his arrival with his small band of followers, Saint Mungo heard from the people that this new pope was a very holy man and was to be known as Pope Gregorius (Gregory) I. He was also nicknamed 'Golden Mouth', as his sermons on the Scriptures were so clear and easily understood. Saint Mungo had many audiences with Pope Gregorius and was given instructions for the development of the faith. Fortified by a new inner resolve received from Pope Gregorius, Saint Mungo made his plans to return home, in the knowledge of faith shown in him by the Holy Father. As a parting gift, Pope Gregorius gave Saint Mungo some relics of past saints and some ornaments to adorn the altar of his beloved church in Glashgu. One other gift the Pontiff had commissioned for him was a special blessed bell to be hung in his church and to ring so that the area around Glashgu would know that Christ's blessings are on those who follow his teachings.

When Mungo arrived back on home soil, word spread fast over the kingdom. In anticipation of the homecoming of their beloved bishop, plans were set down for a great celebration throughout the land. The people had organised an entourage to travel down the road to escort Mungo home in the manner fitting one who is loved by the Almighty Lord above all earthly men. As they entered the township of Glashgu the returning monks rang out the pontiff's holy bell, letting the people know that they were not alone but part of the universal Church. They were the children of the Lord and would always be well favoured by the Holy Father in Rome. This bell would signify that peace and prosperity had come to the land.

To the north around this time, in the year AD 592, Abbot Columba had just completed a successful mission in the Picts' land. On his way back to his abbey on the island of Iona, as the Lord would have it, he was brought into close proximity to the Cambrian kingdom. His longing for a meeting with Mungo, after hearing all the great deeds and miracles he had done in the Lord's name, made him stop. He had an overwhelming desire to look the man of God in the eyes and rejoice in the light of his holiness. Now he thought was the time, as both were growing old and this chance might never present itself again. He ordered his disciples to turn south, and to head towards the holy ground where Mungo had made his home.

Dividing his disciples into three groups, he started on this journey that his scribes would record for posterity. All the way they chanted psalms and called out their prayers so that all who could hear would know that a man of the Lord was passing by. He also sent on ahead a messenger to inform Saint Mungo that the imminent arrival of Columba was near. At hearing this news, Mungo's heart was lifted. Here was a man he had heard about and admired for many years – making a pilgrimage to see him. He assembled all his disciples, arranging them into three groups: in the front he placed the juniors; next he placed those more advanced in years; lastly he placed those according to the length of service to the Lord. Saint Mungo himself walked in the front of the last group, and the procession went out to meet with the oncoming holy man, singing psalms as they walked. As they neared one another they could hear each other's chants, Saint Columba's party sang out, 'Your saints shall go from strength to strength, until your God of gods appears, every one, in Sion.'

One of the monks with Columba asked him if the holy man, Mungo, would be in the first group. He answered, 'Neither the first group or the second group will he be in, but where you see a fiery pillar above and a crown on his head you will know it is he.'

Closer they came and from Mungo's group could be heard, 'In the ways of the Lord how great is the glory of the Lord'; Columba's disciples answered, 'The way of the just is made straight, and the path of the saints prepared.'

When the two saints met they threw their arms around each other and bathed in the holiness that the Lord God had bestowed on them. The joy of the groups was in seeing the love each had for one another. A heavenly glow enveloped them and the Lord looked down and was pleased that his two chosen sons had found such pleasure in each other. This was a hallowed place for this meeting, consecrated by Saint Ninian all those years ago only to have the most memorable meeting take place of two of our most celebrated saints who left a lasting impression on the land.

Over the next few days the two saints were never apart for too long, as they immersed themselves in matters of the faith. They were deep in admiration for all they had done in the Lord's name. The closeness between these two saints was reflected by the closeness between the Christian kings, Rydderck and the Scots king, Aidan. As we have seen in the past, they had fought together to rid their kingdoms of paganism. It was through the Lord's guiding hand that Columba counselled these two kings before they went into battle, the outcome of which would make the way open for these two saints to fulfil the promise of the Lord.

As the two saints were so engrossed in each other's company, some of the weaker-willed converts of Columba began to doubt this holy man, Mungo, whose name was on everyone's lips as the saint who worked all the miracles. It was said of him that he restored sight to the blind; to the deaf he gave back their hearing; to the dumb he loosened their tongues so they could speak; to the diseased of limb he gave the will to walk again. But these converts had not seen these things happen. Disregarding the tales because of their poor faith, they became bored. As all thieves do who are born to this way of life, they slipped away to the fields where was kept the flock of sheep belonging to the holy church of Mungo.

The shepherd, seeing these men of poor morals trying to steal a sheep, said to them, 'Ask of the holy bishop, Mungo, and he would give to you the choice you wished of these beasts.'

Ignorant men that they were, they overpowered the shepherd and slew the fattest ram in the herd by cutting off its head. Then, chasing the shepherd away, they sat down to deliberate where they should skin the beast.

As they sat contemplating, something amazing happened before their eyes. The headless ram stood up and ran back into the field, whereupon it collapsed. One of the men had an even more startling experience; the head of the ram he was holding turned to stone and stuck fast to his hands. The thieves decided to scamper away, but the one whose hands were stuck to the head of the ram pleaded with them to take him to the holy bishop.

'Was it not said that he was the only one who could set me free by his miracles?' said the luckless man. The others agreed to the wishes of their comrade. Sheepishly entering into the monastery, they threw themselves at Mungo's feet. With tears in their eyes, they pleaded with him to forgive them their evil intentions and release their friend from the curse that had befallen him. Mungo saw into their hearts and knew they were sincere. He rebuked them and forgave them. He set the man free from his affliction and told them they were free to return to their homes. Kissing Mungo's feet, they praised him for his mercy.

Mungo said to them 'It is not I you should praise for forgiveness, but the Almighty Lord, for it is He who forgives all sins.'

As they left, he told them to take away with them the slaughtered carcass of the ram they had so desired.

Having spent so many days talking about ways to further the Lord's work, the time finally came for the two saints to take their leave of one another. A mass celebrated by the two saints to partake in spiritual food for the soul took place. During the mass the saints exchanged their holy pastoral staves. The staff Columba received from Mungo was a symbol of the passing on of the Lord's cloak of protection. It is said that from that moment on, Saint Mungo started to feel the bite of the worldly weather around him. Saint Columba, it is said, would soon travel into the heart of the Pict kingdom of the Grampians and convert the Pict king. The staff the Lord had prepared for Mungo would protect Columba from the heathen hordes.

That night a banquet was held for the partaking of bodily food. The next morning it was time to say their farewells. As he watched them go away, singing psalms as they walked, Mungo thought to himself he had never seen such a sad and glorious sight as he had seen that day.

Mungo kept Columba's staff until the end of his days, and it supported him in his old age as his bones began to punish him. It is also said that this staff, after the passing of Saint Mungo, found its way into the safe keeping of the Church of Saint Wilfred, bishop and confessor at Ripon. It was held here in great reverence, on the account of the holy meeting when it passed hands between two great saints.

The Molendinar area must be one of the most blessed of places in Scotland. Three of our most revered saints, Saint Ninian, Saint Mungo and Saint Columba, at some time in their lives were there for a while. No other area in Scotland can boast of this unique trilogy of saints.

Saint Columba's soul departed his body in the year AD 597. Saint Mungo, it is said, knew of his passing from this life. Of the miracle of the ram's head, it was said that the stone head was kept in the monastery church for a long time and can still be seen today in the same spot.

The Final Journey

Only the pure in spirit do not fear death, for they have been told by the Lord Jesus that they will enter into heaven. So it was with Saint Mungo in his last days on earth. Even though his body was wracked with pain of old age, he did not complain. This he accepted as the will of the Lord as penance for all the good things the Lord had done for him in this life.

He didn't even complain when he had an affliction of his jaw, and it is said that the hinges of his jaws became defunct and his jaw would drop down. Feeling his disciples might be upset by seeing his gaping mouth, he tied a bandage around his head and jaws so that he had support.

In his later years he was still of a good mind, still managed to give council to all who were in need, and his wisdom was a gift that came down from the Lord. Right up till his body would no longer carry him, he had participated in the solemn mass to celebrate the holy mysteries of the Lord. When his body could no longer carry him, he would be carried in and laid at the foot of the altar so that he could still be present on these solemn occasions and receive the sacraments of the body and blood of Our Lord Jesus Christ.

This period was a trying time for his faithful followers, as they had always relied on the wisdom of the holy Bishop Mungo whenever they were in need of guidance. As Mungo's condition deteriorated, the mood of the entire monastery changed. Mungo had visitations from angels and was in a state of grace when his beloved disciples called for the Lord to restore their most holy bishop back to good health. To some, life without him would be unthinkable.

Mungo could feel their sorrow and said to them, 'I am not long for this world, but do not be afraid, for the Father in heaven will give to you the strength to carry on. Stay by all I have taught you of the Lord Jesus and always stay true to yourselves. Never accuse, but always forgive, and the Lord will always be by your side.'

As the day and the hour drew near, the Devil tried to persuade the holy man that it was he, the Devil himself, who had watched over him all these years. It was his God who had deserted him and was even now inflicting him with all this pain in his old age.

The Devil said to him, 'If the Lord is so good, why is he punishing you even now, right up till the breath leaves your body? He should be rewarding you for the faith you have shown in him by removing all this pain.'

Saint Mungo prayed to the Lord to take away these evil thoughts that the Devil was trying to put in his mind, to restore to him the peace that he had had before. The Lord, hearing his faithful servant's prayer, banished from his mind these evil thoughts, replacing them with the sounds of the voices of the monks singing psalms in the chapel.

Those who were attending him asked if he would intercede to the Lord on their behalf that they could join him on his celestial journey to heaven, for they wished to follow him as they had through life. Tiring, Saint Mungo said to them, 'May God's will be done, if it be His wish that you should accompany me on this journey. May He dispose of us as He best pleases.'

At this he fell silent, as if in communion with the angels. Watching over him, they saw a heavenly glow surround his body, and knew his time was drawing near. Tears of grief for their dear saint washed away their sins, cleaning their souls. The angel appeared before those assembled, so bright their eyes could not take in the sight; dropping to their knees they all bowed their heads in prayer, afraid to look lest they be blinded.

Mungo no longer felt the pain of old age. With body and soul, all his thoughts were of when he would be with the Lord in heaven.

The angel, hovering over Mungo, said to him, 'Command your disciples tomorrow to prepare a bath. Fill it with warm water so that you might step in and with your pain all gone you will fall into a sleep in the Lord. If it be your desire the Lord grants for you those who would join you on your journey out of your body and into heaven, but only those who are at peace with all things on earth, and have paid all debts to nature.' At this the angel faded away and his voice was no longer heard, as if it had been some wonderful dream. Saint Mungo wakened and, cured of all his afflictions, he sat up on his couch.

Speaking to his disciples of all the angel had revealed to him, he commanded them that a bath prepared with warm water should be made ready next day, as the Lord had commanded. He then explained to them all that had been said by the angel on the matter of those who wished to follow him into heaven, to join with Him who is the Lord of all life. They who did follow, he told them, must enter into the bath of water while the warmth was still there. Saint Mungo also told them that only the pure in spirit would be allowed to make the journey with him. Those who were not would be cast back and suffer a punishment from the Lord for having presumed that anyone impure would be granted entrance into the Kingdom of Heaven. At this he sent them away to prepare all that had been commanded.

All night long his beloved disciples prayed to the Lord to lift all their sins from their souls, that they might join with the holy bishop on his last journey, a journey that would last for ever with the Lord. The next morning, having prepared themselves and the bath of warm water, they escorted their beloved saint on his last earthly journey to the place that housed the bath. After deliberation, some felt that they were far from ready to meet their maker and decided that they would better serve the Lord by staying in their earthly bodies. Some, though, were pure of heart and soul and were chosen by the Lord to accompany their beloved bishop.

On the day of the Lord's Epiphany, 13 January 603, Mungo entered into the room unaided, being free of all human weaknesses. Blessing all those around him, he said, 'My time here on earth is now over. I now go to be with the Father in heaven. What the Lord has given to me I bequeath to you. Faith is a very sacred thing and must be nurtured at all times; do not be afraid when times are bad, as the Lord will always triumph in the end. My legacy I leave to you is faith that you trust in the Lord, hope that the Lord in his mercy will give to you an abundance of all that is good, and, lastly, charity: as you would have your fellow men treat you, you should do to them the same but twofold. Until we meet again in heaven I leave you my blessings.'

Watching as their beloved saint stepped into the bath, they saw at each end of the bath two angels dressed in gold appear. They were sent by the Lord to escort Mungo to his celestial home in heaven. Lying down in the warm water in the bath, he quickly fell asleep, a deep sleep through which no more of the strains of life would torture him. The disciples watching saw Mungo's spirit rise up in all his glory from his earthly prison of a body to join the angels. Amazed, they stood watching as the three joined together in praise of the Almighty God. A beacon of light of one, who was their saviour on earth, had gone out of their lives and uncertainty would roam the land. The disciples who had chosen to share in this glory lifted the body that had been their bishop, laying his shell of a body on a couch, and, one by one, they stepped into the bath – quickly, lest the water turned cold. Each, in turn, fell into a sleep where their souls were released from their bodies, and, freed, they joined their beloved bishop to journey with him on his last mission.

With due respect in time honoured to grieve over the loss of their most holy leader, preparations for the interment of the holy bones of Saint Mungo that remained on earth took place. Celebrating the religious rites of care and devotion, Saint Mungo's remains were placed in a cask and interred at the right-hand corner of the high altar in the manner befitting a bishop who was a saint of those days. The bodies of the disciples who had desired to join with Saint Mungo were interred in the monastery graveyard in the order they had left this life. Folklore has it that over 650 holy monks lie buried in the graveyard.

In the year of Saint Mungo's death, Rydderck was killed in the Battle of Daegsastan. The pagan king, Ethelfrith, established his throne, which saw a period of darkness return to the Cambrian kingdom. The pagan armies swept all before them, fighting a battle on the braes of Hawkhill in Alloa before brushing all aside until King Ethelfrith was slain nearly fourteen years later in a great battle in AD 617. Then, once again, Christianity flourished throughout the land, as Saint Mungo had foretold.

After spending eighty-five years at the Lord's call, it was fitting

The crypt of Saint Mungo.
© *Crown Copyright. Reproduced courtesy of Historic Scotland.*

that Saint Mungo's death should have been as gentle as lying down to sleep on a warm sunny day. The legacy of faith he left for us is still as true today as it was then; Saint Mungo always trusted the Lord and the Lord never let him down. He was a true martyr for his faith throughout his life; and always ready to face death for his Saviour. He continually did penance even if the need was not there. Some say he was an angel of the Lord sent down to show the way to the truth. It is also said he was a prophet of the Lord, for he was privy to things of the future, and always laid bare the future to those who would listen. Throughout his life he suffered the envy of others in silence, but still triumphed over those who would persecute him. Never did he condemn those who sinned, but was always willing to forgive, even to the point of doing their penance himself. He was truly a son of God.

Children were taught in Glasgow of the miracles of Saint Mungo. One of the rhymes they learnt was:

> Here is a bird that once flew,
> Here is a tree that once grew,
> Here is a bell that once rang,
> Here is a fish that once swam.

In honour of one of the holiest of dedicated bishops, Saint Mungo (Kentigern), a magnificent cathedral stands on the spot where he established his first monastery, by the side of the Molendinar Burn nearly 1,460 years ago. Out of the deep faith he put down, there flourished around it a vibrant city, known today as Glasgow. Many miracles were said to have taken place around our venerable saint's place of rest, whose holy relics, it is said, lie within the walls of the hallowed cathedral that grew up over the centuries.

The present cathedral has gone through many changes over the centuries, becoming more and more grand, even surviving the onslaught of time and the Reformation around 1560. During the Reformation a lot of our religious and historical heritage was lost for ever. Wanton destruction of the interior has left the cathedral bare of all the religious artefacts of the Roman Catholics. All over Scotland the same thing happened, until hardly a written word was left of what had gone before. We will never know the real truth of all that went before this period. But one thing is certain: we have lost much knowledge of the times when saints like Mungo walked this land, and laid down the seeds of Christianity.

Saint Mungo's Cathedral, Glasgow.

Select Bibliography

Books, Pamphlets and Articles

Beveridge, David, *Culross and Tulliallan*, vol. 1, Edinburgh and London, William Blackwood and sons, 1885

Bryson, Rev. A, 'Alloa and Tullibody', in Maclean Watt, L [ed], *Alloa and Tullibody*, Alloa, 1902.

Capaldi, I G, SJ, *Tales of Kentigern*, Scotland, Nunraw Abbey, 1995

Cooper, Rev. James, DD, 'Three Fathers of the Faith in Scotland', in Maclean Watt, L [ed], *Alloa and Tullibody*, Alloa, 1902.

Fawcett, Richard, *Glasgow Cathedral*, Edinburgh, Historic Scotland, 1997

Forbes, Alexander Penros, DCL, *Lives of Saint Ninian and Saint Kentigern*, Edinburgh, Edmondston and Douglas, 1874

Gordon, Rev. T Crouther, *A Short History of Alloa*, Alloa, 1937

——, *History of Clackmannan*, Alloa, 1936

Hastings, James, 'Saint Mungo', *Catholic Life*, July 2003

King, Elspeth, *Saint Mungo Patron Saint of Glasgow*, Glasgow Museum and Art Galleries, 1984

Mackay, George, *Scottish Place Names*, Lomond, 2000

Metcalfe, W M, DD [trans.], *Ancient Lives of Scottish Saints*, Paisley, A Gardner, 1895

Rees, Elizabeth, *Celtic Saints in their Landscapes*, Stroud, Sutton, 2001

Stephen, W, *History of Scottish Church*, Edinburgh, David Douglas, 1894

Yule, John, *Natural Science and Archaeology*, Alloa, 1866

Websites

'Saint David, Patron Saint of Wales',
  http://www.Wales-calling.com/culture/st-david.htm

'Saint Kentigern, First Bishop of Glasgow', *The Orthodox Church in America*, http://www.oca.org

'Saint Asaph Cathedral', *Denbigh in Denbighshire*,
  http://www.denbigh.com/asaph.html

'The Age of Saints', http://www.temlum.freeserve.co.uk

'History of the Scottish Nation', http://www.electricscotland.com

'Cumbria: The Age of Kings',
  http://www.zensurweb.com/darkage/ timeline.htm

'Saint Mungo's Church', http://www.saintmungo.org

'Saint Kentigern', *Catholic Encyclopaedia*
  http://www. newadvent.org

Glasgow City Crest, http://www.glasgow.gov.uk

Printed in the United Kingdom
by Lightning Source UK Ltd.
119239UK00001B/148-195